Contents

CONTENTS

Introduction

Only one thing is certain in business. If the owners want to take out more than they put in, they have to make profits. Profits are not an optional extra. They are both the key to your success, and the measure of that success.

Of course, making profits is not easy. It takes a great deal of hard work. Remember, the only place that *profit* comes before *work* is in the dictionary. This book has been written for the managers and owner-managers of small and medium-size businesses who are prepared to work at improving their profits.

The book takes you on a guided tour through the obvious ways of improving your profits – increasing your sales and reducing your costs. It also looks at the less obvious areas, including how to set your prices, how to manage your assets, how to get the most out of your professional advisers and how to get something for nothing.

Although there are more than 101 ideas to improve your profits within these pages, they are inevitably only a selection of the thousands I could have included. Some will be startling. Some will be familiar. Some will be so obvious that you will wonder why you never thought of them. They should all be thought provoking. They should all make you ask: What do we do now? How can we do it better? When do we start?

Supercharge Your Sales and Marketing

Accountants are sometimes criticised for not understanding enough about what makes businesses tick. There might even be some truth in the criticism. But on one point, at least, we accountants do seem to have got it right. The first piece of information produced in every set of accounts is how much the company has sold. Without those sales there can be no profits.

If you run a business you have to be a salesman. You have to sell yourself to your financial backers, your ideas to your staff, and your products to your customers. This chapter looks at some practical steps you can take to boost your sales.

Way 1   Offer whatever the customers want

It is almost impossible to sell what you want to sell, but it is very easy to sell what your customer wants to buy. Find out what your customers actually want and, if necessary, redesign and repackage your product so that it is exactly what they require. If you get this right, you'll have no problems with sales.

This process of making sure that you supply what the market wants is not a one-off exercise. You must do it continually, both by means of market research and by listening and responding to the individual needs of each customer at every stage of your dealings with them. Sometimes you will have to physically change your products, but quite often it will be enough to change the emphasis in the way they are presented. For example, many household products now emphasise that they are 'environmentally friendly'. In many cases the product hasn't changed. The marketing professionals have simply listened to public concerns, and have carefully re-presented and repackaged their products accordingly.

If your business involves person-to-person selling you can become even more sophisticated, individually tailoring your presentation for each customer. To do this you must make sure that at the start of your 'sales-pitch' you ask probing questions, listen carefully to the responses, and identify exactly what the customer needs and values. You can then adapt your sales presentation exactly to their needs, emphasising the features and benefits you have established are most important to them. How often have you wasted a sales opportunity because you stuck to a rigid sales presentation that didn't reflect what the customer had already told you he or she wanted?

Way 2   Concentrate on existing customers

If your sales team spends most of its time working flat out to find new customers, the chances are they are overlooking a simple home truth. In almost every case, the easiest people to sell to are your existing customers. Nurture and pamper them. They are probably your business's biggest asset. By working hard at your relationship with them, you can turn your one-off *customers* into regular *clients*, and casual sales into repeat business.

One useful technique to nurture client relationships is to regularly send key customers a relevant press cutting on some issue of interest to them and their business. You should also attach a short handwritten note saying something like, 'Just in case you missed it, I thought that you might find this of interest'. Not only does this show a keen and personal interest in their business, but it also keeps your name on the tip of their tongue.

If you really want to impress a major existing or potential client, it is possible to go one step further. You can obtain systematic summaries of *all* the UK's major press stories relating to a particular industry, company or named individual, by using one of the widely available news databases. The information you obtain can then be used to:

• Bring you up to speed on the topical issues affecting your client

- Demonstrate that you have a thorough and enthusiastic interest in their business, or even perhaps
- Establish your business as experts in *their field*, by providing them with a running summary and commentary on the issues affecting their industry.

Unfortunately, these services are not cheap, and therefore you will probably only want to use them for major accounts. Organisations offering these databases include FT Profile (0932 761444) and the Business Research Centre (071–873 3000). Many regional libraries can also access the information on your behalf.

Way 3   Reap the referrals

Referrals are the cheapest and usually the most potent form of marketing for a small business. You should actively seek them out. They are too important to be left to chance.

Encourage your customers to refer you and your business to their contacts. In fact, why not ask them for the names of any other people they know who might be interested in your service/product? Once you've got referrals, don't waste them. Follow them up promptly, politely and relentlessly.

Offering a reward for referrals can help, but don't simply offer discounts or cash as the reward. Ten pounds in discounts or cash costs you £10 in profit. It is much better to give away a £10 reward that only costs you, say, £4. The way to achieve this is to make the reward one of your products or services. Better still, make it something that the person making the referral doesn't usually buy. In this way the reward will be worth much more to the customer than it actually costs you, and by giving away something they wouldn't usually buy you are not under-mining your normal sales. They may even like it so much that they become a regular buyer of the new product as well!

Way 4   Get more from every opportunity

Here are just three things you can do to generate a higher level of sales from every sales opportunity:

1. *Repeat business.* Make sure that you get repeat business by rewarding customers for their loyalty.

   A major supermarket recently ran a very successful loyalty campaign. Every £10 spent with them in November and December earned points that could be exchanged for vouchers to be spent over Christmas. The scheme was cleverly designed so that the points could only be redeemed in multiples of ten. Once you started saving the points, you went back week after week to make sure that you reached the next multiple of ten. The redemption period was also strictly limited (from about 20 December to New Year's Eve). As a result the cost of the promotion was kept down because a lot of the shoppers who avidly collected their points never actually redeemed them. Could you do something similar to encourage repeat purchases by your customers?

2. *Product range.* Extend your product range to include complementary services such as installation, training, technical support, servicing, repairs and extended warranties. If you don't have the resources to provide all these services yourself, subcontract out the work to somebody who can.

   The same principle can also be applied to complementary products. For example, many video hire shops now also sell popcorn and confectionery because customers like to buy nibbles when hiring a video.

3. *Offer more.* We all know that you can lead a horse to water, but you can't make it drink. What the proverb doesn't say is that if you don't lead your horse to water it will die of thirst and you will have no transport! The moral for the horse rider is – make sure you *offer* it a drink. The moral for the salesperson is – make sure you offer your customers the chance to buy *more* from you.

   When someone hires a film from your video shop ask them if they would like any popcorn. If you feel really confident, you can even try asking them whether they would like a small or large bag of popcorn with their video. And just when they think they have finished their order, ask: 'Is there anything else sir, perhaps some crisps, chocolates, Coke?' You probably don't run a video business, but the principles are the same: if you don't go out of your way to encourage customers to spend more they won't, and if you do, they might.

Way 5   Commission schemes – the good, the bad and the ugly

If you've got a sales team then you've probably got a commission scheme. Most commission schemes are designed to encourage the salesforce to sell more. No problem so far, you may be thinking. But you are wrong. To be effective a commission scheme should not encourage and reward higher sales volume alone. It must only promote higher sales if they are also *profitable*.

Too many commission schemes reward sales volume with no regard to the price at which those sales are made, or to the profits that they generate. It is the easiest thing in the world for a salesperson to increase sales by cutting prices. Although price cutting may be easy, it is often very unprofitable (see Way 20). If your commission scheme rewards sales volumes without penalising price cutting, you should take a long, hard look at it.

Example
A company buys its products for £7 each and usually sells them for £10. It operates an industry standard commission scheme that gives its sales staff a 10 per cent commission on the total value of sales. A new opportunity has arisen and the sales team reckon that they can increase their sales from 100 to 125 a week by reducing the average selling price from £10 to £9. They work hard to achieve these extra sales since, not only will they increase turnover, but they will also boost their own commission from £100 to £112 a week. Understandably they presume that their actions *must* be in the company's interests. Unfortunately, nothing could be further from the truth. As you can see in the table overleaf, the company's profits will actually *fall* from £200 to £138 a week. By using a badly designed commission scheme, the company inadvertently encourages its staff, acting in good faith, to reduce profits!

A bad commission scheme

	Selling 100 units at £10	Selling 125 units at £9
	£	£
Sales	1000	1125
Deduct: cost of sales at £7 each	(700)	(875)
Gross profit	300	250
Deduct: commission at 10% of sales	(100)	(112)
Total profit	200	138

How should the company redesign its scheme? The simplest way is to link the commissions paid to some measure of profitability. For example, it could pay a 33 per cent commission on the gross profits generated by each salesperson. The sales team would no longer have an incentive to reduce company profits because they are rewarded according to those profits.

There are often two objections to this kind of profit-based commission structure: your company doesn't know the profitability of its products, or you don't want your sales team to know. However, even if these objections are valid, there is nothing to stop you using a variation on the same theme. Instead of using the actual cost, use some notional or estimated value for cost of sales. The closer the notional cost of sales figure you use is to the target selling price, the more the commission system will penalise salesmen who rely on price cutting to make their sales. This is particularly appropriate in markets where there is evidence that extra sales can be generated without significant price reductions.

Are the signals and incentives given by your commission scheme consistent with the profitability of your business?

Way 6   Exports are not a 'quick fix'

All too often companies assume that they can quickly and easily solve all of their domestic problems by becoming exporters.

The reality, of course, is very different. Overseas customers will only buy your products if they are technically suitable for the country; meet all the local safety and quality standards and expectations; are packaged and marketed specifically to meet local needs, tastes, laws and customs; are supported by a local sales and after-sales service team; can be supplied reliably and on time; and are competitively priced and available on acceptable terms. The chances of your existing design, specification, packaging, marketing, distribution, customer support, pricing and terms of trading exactly matching the needs of *any* overseas market are extremely slim. The chances of them meeting the needs of *all* your target markets are lower still.

Before you can even consider exporting, you will have to do rather a lot of *importing*. You will need to import market research and intelligence on local customs, tastes, laws, business practice etc. You will also need to import new skills such as export financing, documentation, transport and distribution. And that is only the start of it.

Although some of the difficulties of exporting may be avoided by using a merchant house or wholesaler, this may not be possible in your particular business. These organisations buy goods for specific customers abroad (such as large stores), and the supplier delivers to them; they undertake all dealings with the overseas customer. In any case, their use will only ever be a partial solution to the problem of exporting.

The full solution takes time, effort and money. Exporting is not a quick fix. It is not an instant solution to low profitability. To succeed in exporting takes planning, attention to detail and perseverance. If you don't have the commitment, resources and cash to do all these things, the best advice anybody can give you is don't even think about exporting. Half-hearted, half-planned export initiatives will be a complete waste of money.

Way 7   Help for exporters

If your business wants to break into exporting, you will need all the help you can get, fortunately there is plenty at hand. The Department of Trade and Industry (DTI) works hard to boost the balance of payments by helping businesses to succeed as exporters. Here are some of the very cost-effective ways that the DTI could help your business:

- The *Enterprise Initiative* can subsidise the cost of developing an export marketing strategy. See Way 92 for further details.
- The *Export Marketing Research Scheme* provides free advice on how to plan your market research, and can give grants to help put those plans into action.
- For a fee of under £300 the Commercial Section of an overseas British Embassy of your choice will spend up to 24 hours researching your market and business prospects in that country, and will provide you with a full written report.
- If you need help finding representatives, agents or distributors, the local British Embassy can also help. For under £300 they will spend up to 24 hours contacting, researching, and recommending suitable representatives.
- The *Overseas Status Report Service* can provide a detailed report on the size, status, facilities and activities of any overseas business. The report will be individually prepared by the British Embassy after they have carried out both desk research and actually visited the business. The cost ranges from £55 to £270, and for this the Embassy will spend up to 24 hours on the project.
- The *New Products from Britain* service will professionally write, translate and distribute a press release to all suitable magazines, papers and journals in the countries of your choice. They'll even provide you with a list of all the places that your story was published. At a fixed fee of only £60 per country, this represents outstanding value for money!
- The DTI has an excellent export reference library in London which can be used free of charge. It also publishes a wide range of very useful free publications.
- The DTI run a 24-hour *Business in Europe Hotline* to answer queries you may have about any aspect of exporting.
- There are also specialist export help desks or units for almost every country, region and market in the world.

You can find out more about any of these services to exporters by ringing either your local office of the DTI, or the *Business in Europe Hotline* on 0272 444888.

Way 8   Tips for exporters

A whole book could be written on how to run an export operation profitably. Here are just four ideas that could save money or help to avoid costly mistakes.

1. Don't appoint the first overseas agent or distributor who shows an interest in your products. Whoever you appoint will be a key business partner, so make sure you carefully research and consider your options. Once you have appointed somebody, never give them formal sole distribution rights until they have proved their worth. Offer them a six-month trial with *informal* sole distribution rights. If they don't come up to scratch you can walk away at no cost.
2. Many exporters spend sleepless nights worrying about which currency to use for their prices, and whether to quote ex-works prices (ie the price at the manufacturer's factory gate) or delivered prices (ie where the exporter arranges and pays for the delivery to the customer's factory gate). The answer is to find out what your customers prefer and how your competitors operate, and make sure you offer the same or better. In Europe this will probably mean invoicing in your customer's local currency and taking full responsibility for delivery.
3. Twenty per cent of UK exporters use Letters of Credit to ensure that they are paid on time. But be warned, Letters of Credit can be very expensive in both bank charges and administrative effort, and for sales of less than about £4000 they may not be cost effective. Find out the costs and try to build them into your selling price. If you can't increase your prices, investigate other forms of payment protection such as documentary collections, factoring or credit insurance.
4. Export documentation can be a headache. Fortunately the Government's Simpler Trade Procedures Board (SITPRO) has designed a range of document systems that can cut the cost of export paperwork by as much as 75 per cent. SITPRO, who can be contacted on 071-287 3525, will also

provide free advice on any aspect of exporting, including VAT, Customs and Excise procedures and the Single Market.

Way 9   Perfect the art of Pareto

The Pareto principle says that 20 per cent of your efforts will bring 80 per cent of your rewards. For example, 20 per cent of your customers will generate 80 per cent of your sales. Another 20 per cent, not necessarily the same customers, will generate 80 per cent of your profits. Your business efforts will be more rewarding if you work out which customers fall into the most profitable 20 per cent group, and focus your energies and efforts in their direction.

To do this you will need to list all your customers in descending order of annual sales. You should also produce a similar list for your potential customers. Then think about the profitability of each of these accounts. Obviously this will be easy if your management accounting systems analyse customer profitability. If they don't, you will need to look at factors such as sales prices, discounts, payment terms, distribution arrangements and manufacturing costs. You should also consider whether any of your existing small customers have the potential to become big customers, and take this into account.

The aim of the exercise is to estimate the annual profits you earn from each actual customer, and could earn from each potential customer. Your sales team can then focus their time and energies on the:

- Twenty per cent of your customers who currently earn you 80 per cent of your profits;
- Twenty per cent of your smaller customers with the greatest potential to become big customers; and
- Twenty per cent of your sales prospects who would generate the most profits if they became customers.

You should also do a similar analysis of your product range. The Pareto principle says that 80 per cent of your profits come from 20 per cent of your product range. Analyse the profitability of your existing product lines, and concentrate your efforts and energies on the key 20 per cent.

Way 10   Prune the garden

There is another important implication of the Pareto principle. The 80 per cent of your customers and products that do least for your profitability also probably account for the vast majority of your queries, complaints, returns, disputes and bad debts. When the true costs of all of these factors are taken into account, those products and customers may actually be doing you more harm than good.

As every gardener knows, it is sometimes necessary to severely prune some parts of a garden to enable the rest of it to flourish. Too many businesses persist with loss-making products or customers, sometimes out of a misplaced sense of loyalty or optimism, but more usually out of ignorance as to their true cost to the rest of the business. Sort out the flowers from the weeds in your garden, and start pruning!

Way 11   Quality, quality, quality

Quality has become the buzzword of the decade. It seems to me that there are two key aspects to the quality revolution:

• Getting it right first time, every time; and

• Being *recognised* for getting it right first time, every time.

It is no longer enough to *detect* poor quality using traditional quality control techniques. The key to getting it right the first time is to *prevent* poor quality happening at all. This means building excellence into every step of the process, into every aspect of the business. Of course, this is very much easier said than done.

One much publicised place to start is BS 5750. This is an internationally recognised standard for quality management systems. But this is only the *start*. The quest for total quality is, in reality, a never-ending journey. If you've already embarked on the journey, don't stop at BS 5750. Worthy though it is, it is only a milestone, and an optional one at that. The key is to keep on striving for quality, not just today and tomorrow, but always. If you don't get things right the first time, it costs time and money to do them again. In fact, it probably costs you much more than just money: staff motivation, product reliability, customer goodwill and satisfaction and the reputation of your business will all be seriously damaged.

As the 1990s unfold your customers will expect ever higher quality standards from your business. In tomorrow's marketplace, if you have to keep saying 'Sorry', the chances are your customers will say start to say 'Goodbye'. Is your business paying lip service to quality, or are you *really* doing something about it?

Way 12 Complaints as an opportunity, not a threat

How do you react to customer complaints? Is your natural response to grit your teeth and grudgingly acknowledge that you were wrong? Properly handled, complaints and dissatisfaction are an opportunity, not a threat. How? Quite simply, they are an opportunity to so overwhelm complainants with your response that they become your best customers, and your most profitable source of referrals.

Example
Office products suppliers Viking Direct are one company who have made a virtue out of complaints. They do not charge for any item that you try for 30 days and decide, for whatever reason, you don't like. And they will refund, at any time within a year of purchase, the full cost of anything that doesn't work the way it should. What's more, in both cases they will even come and collect the rejected items within 24 hours of the complaint.

We buy all our office supplies from Viking, and so far have had no reason to complain about any of their products. But even if I did have cause to complain, I am sure that I would continue to buy from them and continue to mention their unique service to my clients. Viking have succeeded in making me a champion of their cause. Could your business turn complaints into opportunities, and customers into champions of your cause?

Way 13   Double your advertising budget

If you've heard it once, you've probably heard it a thousand times: half of all advertising is wasted, the problem is that you don't know which half! But do you really need to worry about it? Not if you can *halve* the cost of advertising, or *double* its effectiveness! Simple arithmetic tells me that if an advert only costs me half what I expected it to, then I don't need to worry too much if half of it is wasted. So how can you make your advertising budget go twice as far?

- Choose your newspapers carefully. Look at the types of business that advertise in them. There is usually safety in numbers, so if nobody else in your industry advertises in a particular paper then you probably shouldn't either. Ask your customers which papers they read, and how they found out about you, and start to draw up a shortlist.

- Look at the cost. Not just the total cost of placing an advert, but the effective cost per thousand readers. A slightly more expensive advert in a high circulation free paper is often much better value than a cheaper advert in a 'paid for' paper: the cost per thousand readers will probably be lower and, for many businesses, the response rate in free papers is much higher.

- Meet the advertising representatives from the papers on your shortlist. Ask them to make up proofs for two or three adverts of different sizes, including one very large one that you can't actually afford! Most papers will do this free of charge. Compare the proofs produced by each paper, and then sit back and wait.

- As the paper gets closer to its copy deadline, it will become more and more desperate to sell its remaining advertising space. Since it knows that you are a potential advertiser, and that you already have camera ready proofs, it will ring you up offering discount prices. The closer it gets to the print deadline, the easier it will be for you to negotiate even bigger discounts.

- A good advert can lose much of its impact if it appears on a page with little or no editorial. Expensive half-page adverts often find themselves sharing a page with another half-page advert, and as a result are often turned over unread. Try a vertical advert of, say, 28cm deep by five columns wide. This size will cost about the same as a half-page, but because of its shape it is guaranteed to be the largest advert on a page in a tabloid paper. It is also likely to be surrounded by editorial rather than other adverts.

- Make sure that you see the finished advert as soon as it is published. Typographical errors do happen but, not surprisingly, the publishers are unlikely to own up to them. By being on the ball you at least have a chance of minimising the damage, and getting the advert reprinted at no cost.

- Monitor the responses carefully. You need to know which adverts and which publications gave you the greatest responses. Ask new customers how they found out about you, and systematically record, monitor and *learn* from their answers.

- And finally, there is no point in spending money on advertising or any other form of promotion if the sales leads it generates are wasted. Make sure that you are able to handle any level of response, from a trickle to a flood.

Way 14   What's wrong with this advert?

There is little point in negotiating a brilliant deal on advertising rates if your advert is hopeless. Don't be the judge and jury on your own advertising material – test it before you use it. Try it out on friends, colleagues and customers. Does it grab their attention? Is it easy to read and understand? Does it emphasise the benefits rather than the features of your product or service? Does it contain the information necessary for the reader to act (phone number, address, reply coupon etc)?

The acid test is to ask 'I wonder if you can see what's wrong with this, we've only just noticed it ourselves!' There may not be an error, of course, but you can bet that it will receive a very thorough, independent examination – and if there is something wrong, they will find it.

Way 15   What's news?

If you can't afford to advertise, or you don't feel it is appropriate for your business, you can still appear in the papers. Newspapers and magazines need *news* as well as advertising. Over the last 12 months I have managed to get my business into the local papers over 30 times, and I haven't paid a penny for the privilege. If I can achieve that amount of free publicity for a business as apparently dull as accountancy, how much more coverage could your business generate?

I am willing to bet that there are five to ten stories somewhere in your organisation at this very moment. They might include:

- An unusual enquiry to sell sand to Saudi Arabia
- The appointment, promotion or retirement of a member of your staff
- Your imminent move to new premises
- Your involvement with a local charity or good cause
- An unusual hobby or pastime of one of your employees
- Your caring approach to the environment
- A visit from a prominent person
- Your sponsorship of a local event
- Giving local schoolchildren a guided tour of your factory
- Offering work experience to a local youngster
- Awards or prizes that you, your business or its employees have won
- Winning a major new customer, sale or contract
- Launching a new product or service.

The list is almost endless!

What journalists will not do is to give you a blatant plug when there is nothing newsworthy about your story. But almost every story has a news angle. You just have to find it. A familiar example will help to illustrate the news angles that can be found or created in seemingly mundane circumstances.

Example
Smallco has just launched a new product, the Plugger. Some of the news angles on this story could include:

- 'Revolutionary new product could create 20 new jobs in Ourtown';
- 'Local firm set to put Ourtown on the map with its revolutionary Plugger which could see orders pouring in from all over the world'; and
- 'Lucky Ourtown schoolchildren have been given a unique insight into business. John Smith, managing director of Smallco, gave 10 keen youngsters a guided tour of his factory on Thursday. He explained what was involved in designing and manufacturing their world beating products, including the revolutionary new Plugger.'

Here's another example that worked for me. When I took on my first assistant my business doubled its staff number overnight (from one to two!). Not very newsworthy you might

Expansion taken into account . . .

CHARTERED accountants Stephens & Co reckon their expansion plans could have an interesting impact on the local economy.

On September 1 they not only opened a new office in Welwyn Garden City, but also doubled in size by taking on qualified accountant Carol Walmsley (30) of Panshanger.

Founder of the business, Steve Pipe told the *Mercury*: "If we carry on doubling our staff numbers each day, we will employ the entire population of Hertfordshire by September 20 and the entire country before the end of the month. After that, the sky's the limit."

To mark the occasion the company is offering local small businesses a free 25-page guide on how to succeed in the current climate. Copies can be obtained by ringing 0707 328432.

think. But I managed to get coverage in all my local papers by spotting an amusing angle. It just takes a little imagination!

Think about your business, talk to your staff, customers and suppliers. How many stories and news angles can you come up with?

Way 16   Press releases

Journalists can't write about your business and its stories unless they know about them. How do they find out? Its quite simple really – *you tell them*. The easiest way is to send them press releases. A press release is simply a written summary of the key elements of your story: who, what, where, when, how and why?

Here are some of the golden rules of successful press releases:

- Get to know the journalists covering stories in your area, and send your releases direct to them.
- Type them on A4 paper with double spacing and wide margins.
- Use only one side of the paper. If you need more space, continue on a separate sheet and staple them together.
- Make it short, simple and snappy. Use short sentences, and keep it to one or two sheets of A4 paper.
- Don't use jargon.
- Clearly state that it is a 'Press Release' at the top of the first page.
- Give it a simple headline that says what the story is about. But don't be surprised if the journalist writes his own. After all, that's what they are paid for.
- Date it.
- The first paragraph should capture the imagination and cover all the key points of the story. Newspapers go straight to the heart of the story in their opening sentences. Don't leave any new or important facts or issues to the last paragraph. If the

paper is short of space or time they may cut your last paragraph or two.

- Tailor the wording so that it is relevant to the readers of the particular paper or magazine you are dealing with. For example, say 'Local solicitors Hinge & Bracket of Newtown Road . . .' for local press releases, and 'The Newtown office of the international solicitors, Hinge & Bracket . . .' in press releases for a wider audience.

- Include direct quotes from named employees, or even from satisfied customers. These add interest, colour and credibility to the story. They also make the journalist's life a little easier because he won't have to ring you up to get a quote.

- Include a photograph wherever possible. Head and shoulder portrait photos will do, but action photos that illustrate the story are much better.

- At the end of the story type the word 'ENDS' in capital letters.

- Carefully check punctuation, grammar and spelling.

- Give the name, address and phone number of the person the journalists should contact if they want further information.

- Make sure that your press releases are sent out simultaneously to all the relevant publications, and are received well in advance of their copy deadlines.

There are no guarantees that your story will be published. Much will depend on the competition from other news items. A strong story may be squeezed out one week by the sheer weight of hard news. The following week a poor story may get good coverage because nothing else has happened. And even if your story is printed, you may not like what the journalist actually says. Nevertheless, press releases are much cheaper than advertisements, and they can be considerably more effective in promoting your business. Why not give them a try?

Way 17 Press coverage – who reads it?

Today's newspapers are tomorrow's fish and chip wrappers. How can you give your hard-earned press coverage a longer shelf-life? How can you make sure that each and every one of your customers and contacts reads that story about you in an obscure trade journal?

The answer is simple. Keep an attractive presentation file of your press cuttings on the coffee table in your reception area. You might also want to include material from your latest advertising campaign. All your visitors will browse through it as they wait. It will do wonders for your credibility and authority. It may even help to clinch that major contract you have been bidding for!

Way 18   Become a mini-author

How can you get potential customers to read about you if you can't afford to advertise, and you can't persuade journalists to write about your business? One answer is literally staring you in the face – this book. Not everyone will be lucky enough to find themselves published by Kogan Page, but everybody can write and publish something that is helpful to their customers. This book started life as a 25 page word-processed mini-guide that I gave away free of charge. Hundreds of businesses asked for copies, and I gained dozens of clients as a direct result of writing it.

If your business is good at what it does, and if there is a market for your products or services, there will be an audience for an informative and helpful mini-guide to your area of expertise. People will not take much notice of yet another hard-sell sales brochure, but they will want to read a genuinely useful mini-guide. For example, if you sell computers you could write 'The Easy PC Guide to Computers' or a 'Guide to the Data Protection Act'; if you run a playschool you could produce 'How to Choose the Right Childcare'; and if you own a delicatessen, how about recipe booklets for 'The Perfect Dinner Party' and 'The Trouble-free Children's Party'?

Mini-guides like these can provide free publicity, generate new sales leads and help to differentiate your business from its competitors. They demonstrate your expertise and quality, and they enhance your reputation and credibility. In short, they say more about your business and its commitment to its customers than a glossy sales brochure ever can. How many different mini-guides can you write about your business?

Pricing for Profit

It is often said that everything has its price. But how are those prices set? Economists say they are set by the market. They are wrong! You, the business person, choose your own prices. Make the wrong choices and your business suffers. You must live with that responsibility. Do you know what effect your pricing decisions have on your business? How do you set your prices? How *should* you set them? How can you change them?

Way 19   The importance of price

Setting your prices is probably the single most important and difficult decision that you will make for your business.

Most successful smaller businesses realise that they are, or should be, niche players. They understand that to succeed they must deliberately position themselves in the market as suppliers of high quality products or services, providing unparalleled standards of customer support and service, and offering good value for money – at a price that is *fair, not cheap*.

Many unsuccessful small businesses make the mistake of believing that the only way that they can fight for a share of the market is by undercutting their competitors on price. Unfortunately, by doing this they are usually playing to the strengths of their bigger or longer established competitors. The competition usually have deeper pockets, a greater ability to obtain discounts from suppliers, and a base of loyal customers who believe that 'cheap' means 'nasty', and that paying any less than they currently pay *must* involve sacrificing quality.

Don't let your business, however well intentioned the motives, fall into the trap of price undercutting. In almost every industry, being the cheapest in the market will only serve to:

- Reinforce the image of your product or service as 'cheap and nasty';
- Prevent you from winning quality conscious customers; and
- Produce a low sales volume and low profit margin business that will almost inevitably struggle to survive.

The first pricing lesson that every entrepreneur must learn is that low prices should never be the only weapon in your marketing armoury, and that you should never compete on price alone. To succeed you must price for profit.

Way 20   Price for profit

To prove my claim that setting your prices is probably the single most important business decision you make, here's a simple example.

Example
Smallco sells calculators. Last month it made £500 profit selling 1000 units.

Last Month's Profit and Loss Account

	£
Sales (1000 at £10)	10,000
Deduct: cost of sales (1000 at £7)	(7,000)
Gross profit	3,000
Deduct: fixed overheads	(2,500)
Net profit	£500

Smallco has commissioned some market research which suggests that they have two options:

- *Option A* – they could increase their sales volume by 20 per cent if they reduced prices by 10 per cent to £9.

PRICING FOR PROFIT

- *Option B* – they could put up their prices by 10 per cent to £11, but then would lose 10 per cent of their sales volume.

I am willing to bet that your initial reaction when reading these options went something like this: 'Go for Option A. It is always worth selling more, and anyway, Smallco gain more in volume than they are losing in price, so it *must* be profitable.' If this was your reaction, you can take some comfort from the fact that most other readers, and most entrepreneurs, agree with you. Unfortunately, however, the business mathematics show that you are wrong!

Next Month's Profit and Loss Account

	Option A Reduce price	Option B Increase price
	£	£
Sales (A: 1200 at £9 each)	10,800	
(B: 900 at £11 each)		9,900
Deduct: cost of sales		
(A: 1200 at £7 each)	(8,400)	
(B: 900 at £7 each)		(6,300)
Gross profit	2,400	3,600
Deduct: fixed overheads	(2,500)	(2,500)
Net profit/(loss)	£(100)	£1,100

By reducing its prices Smallco is actually worse off: it is worse off than it was before, and it is much worse off than it would have been had it increased its prices.

There is nothing very special or unusual about this example. It simply illustrates a fundamental point that is all too often overlooked: stimulating sales by cutting prices may boost your top line turnover, but can just as easily devastate your bottom line profits.

Smallco will not only be able to generate bigger profits by increasing its prices. By reducing its sales it will also need less cash to finance debtors and stocks, and by eliminating customers at the cheaper end of the spectrum, it will probably reduce the amount of money it loses as bad debts. As a result, under Option B Smallco becomes a leaner, fitter business, providing a higher rate of return using less working capital. Under Option A it becomes a lame duck. Choosing the right pricing strategy can be the difference between success and failure. Is your business an Option A or an Option B company?

There may be occasions when you can *prove* that lower prices will generate higher profits. For example, in the case of Smallco, Option A's 10 per cent price reduction could have been more profitable than Option B's 10 per cent price rise, but *only* if it led to at least an 80 per cent increase in the number of calculators sold!

This illustrates the general rule: if you can prove that the demand for your products is very sensitive to changes in price, then reducing prices may increase your profits. In reality, the demand for products is often much less sensitive to changes in price than we might expect. Convenience, habit, previous satisfaction, concerns over quality, and the 'better the devil you know than the one you don't know' syndrome, all make many customers reluctant to switch allegiance for the sake of a few pence or per cent in price. Try it out on yourself:

• How often do you switch your allegiance from a favourite supermarket, garden centre, pub or restaurant just because a new one has opened up offering slightly lower prices?

• How often do you even realise that they do offer lower prices?

• How often are you prepared to pay just that little bit more for a product or service that you know, understand and are happy with?

I am not suggesting that every business needs to increase its prices. What I am suggesting is that the economics of every pricing decision need to be looked at very closely. Never simply accept the naive equation, much loved by salesmen:

Lower prices = Higher sales = Higher profits

Instead, if you want simple equations, try these two:

Lower prices = Lower profits, until proved otherwise

Higher prices = Higher profits, until proved otherwise

Way 21   How to raise prices

By now you will probably be thinking about whether your business should be raising its prices but are concerned about the customers you might lose. We have already seen many of the reasons why customers probably won't take their custom elsewhere. We have also seen in Way 20 that losing some customers can actually *boost* your profits, and let you run your business with less working capital.

But if you are still a little nervous at the prospect of raising your prices, you'll be pleased to know that there are many ways of raising them that won't cause you to lose too many customers. Here are eight:

1. Tell your customers on a number of occasions that you may have to put up prices by, say, 20 per cent. They will, of course, be 'horrified'. But this horror will turn into an audible sigh of relief when you eventually and triumphantly announce a price rise somewhat below 20 per cent. How far below 20 per cent you pitch the eventual price rise should depend on your assessment of the true depth of their 'horror' when you make the initial suggestion. By making the eventual price rise less painful than your customers were expecting, you can turn a potentially damaging increase into a success.
2. Increase your prices when the rest of your industry does, but by a little more than the industry norm. With any luck you will be able to disguise your higher than average price increase as part of an industry-wide change.

3. Try to reduce the prices of some items in your range at the same time as increasing the prices of most other items. Soften the bad news with some good news, and make a point of dwelling on the latter.

4. Don't increase prices by too much at any one time. On the other hand, don't make small prices rises too often. There is nothing magical or compulsory about annual price rises. In fact, storing up price increases and only changing them once a year means that, when your prices do go up, they get noticed because they are so large. Large price increases will usually be viewed by your customers as unjustified, and will be resisted strongly. On the other hand, in the case of business-to-business sales, anything more frequent than quarterly will cause administrative inconvenience to the buyer, and may be a constant reminder of the fact that your prices are rising while those of your competitors are not. Modestly increasing your prices every six months or so is probably the most sensible compromise.

5. Be prepared to explain why prices have risen, perhaps as a result of cost increases. Also point out that, had it not been for improvements in your own productivity and efficiency, the increase would have been even higher.

6. Better still, explain that the price has increased as a result of improvements to the quality of the product. Emphasise the enhanced features, improved packaging, increased reliability, enhanced customer support, faster and more convenient delivery, and any other factors which make the product better and therefore worth paying more for.

7. Be prepared to justify your prices. It is vital that you have a strong defence prepared in advance. This is likely to include:

   - Knowing the prices of your most expensive competition
   - Demonstrating the savings and benefits from your product
   - Demonstrating that your product is hugely superior and therefore slightly more expensive because . . .
   - Minimising the appearance of the price, for example by talking in terms of the price (in pence?) for each day that the product will be of benefit to them.

8. Finally, and very importantly, look after your major customers. Looking after them doesn't mean exempting them from price increases, but does involve giving them some *temporary* concessions. For example, notify them in advance of the imminent price rise and allow them to stock up at the current prices, or give them a further grace period during which they can purchase at the previous prices.

Way 22   There's no such word as 'can't'

Can't put up your prices? I don't believe it! Try again. Still can't put up your prices? All right, perhaps you are in one of the few markets where the price is as high as it will go. But don't give up yet. You still may be able to introduce some 'non-price' price increases. For example:

- Charging extra for installation, delivery, insurance, handling, storage, etc
- Charging extra for urgent orders or rapid delivery
- Increasing your minimum order size, and introducing a surcharge for any orders below that threshold
- Revising your discount structure
- Slimming down the specification of your product and stripping out any expensive features that are of only limited value to the customer
- Charging interest on overdue accounts.

Way 23   Whose price is it anyway?

Why do we have prices? By publishing a price list businesses run into all sorts of difficulties when they want to change their prices and discounts. In fact, in some businesses it may make more sense not to have a price list at all.

Example
A clothes manufacturer makes men's suits at a cost of £50 each. It can sell 10 a month to a men's outfitter for £150 each, and it can sell another 10 a month to a fashion boutique for £100

each. What price should it set? The worst price it could choose is anything between £101 and £149: at those prices the fashion boutique won't buy any suits, and the outfitters will be able to buy its 10 suits for less than the £150 it is prepared to pay. Here are the profits the manufacturer would earn if it chose *any one of three possible prices*:

Price to all customers	Quantity sold	Sales value	Costs	Profit
£		£	£	£
100	20	2000	1000	1000
125	10	1250	500	750
150	10	1500	500	1000

But why set a single price for all customers? Why not charge the outfitters £150, and charge the boutique £100? As the table below shows, this leads to the highest possible level of profits:

Customer	Price	Qty sold	Sales value	Costs	Profit
	£		£	£	£
Boutique	100	10	1000	500	500
Outfitters	150	10	1500	500	1000
Totals		20	2500	1000	1500

The moral is simple: if you can charge each of your customers the maximum price they are prepared to pay, you will extract every last penny of profit out of your market.

But how can you make this work for your business? First you need to be able divide your customers into groups with similar characteristics. Is your market divided by geography, age or sex? Is it divided between small firms and large multinationals, between new businesses and established businesses, between wholesalers and retailers? Better still, if you only deal with a small number of customers, try to look at each one individually.

The next step is to find out how much each of these customer groups is willing to pay. Look at the prices your competitors charge, talk to your customers, negotiate with them, experiment with different prices and monitor the results.

The final step is to build in safeguards to prevent the lower price customers selling to the high price ones. For a service business this is often straightforward: after all, it is not usually easy for a low price customer to resell the advice, assistance or time that you have supplied to him. Similarly, where the customer groups are based on geography, it may be very difficult or expensive for low price customers to transport and sell your products to high price customers in another country.

Many businesses will have to be more creative. For example, using a different brand image for each customer group, building in technological incompatibilities, introducing customer loyalty schemes, differentiating the higher priced product by adding value and distributing through different types of outlet are just some of the options. But perhaps the easiest method of all is to make it a condition of the sale that the price is kept secret. This won't work in a retail business, but in many other industries it could be worth a try. You might even like to suggest that if the price became common knowledge you would be forced to raise the price across the board.

I can already hear some of you saying, 'We can't do that to our customers'. The truth is you are probably doing it in a limited way already: don't some of your customers already get more discount than others? How much more profit could you earn by throwing out your price list and discounts, and charging customers what they are prepared to pay?

Way 24   Discounts – the forgotten cost

Most smaller businesses don't realise that their single largest cost is one that probably doesn't even appear in their accounts . . . discounts given to customers.

Discounts are a cost in exactly the same way as wages or overheads, and yet even in the largest companies they are often literally 'given away'. Because they have not traditionally been shown in the accounts, they usually escape the control and authorisation procedures that accompany almost every other

cost, and little serious thought is given to their true impli-
cations.

If you are in any doubt about the importance of discounts,
consider for a moment a real example of the simple mathematics of business profits.

Example
A business was having a difficult time. It had already done
everything it could think of to reduce its costs, and yet its
profits were still unacceptably low, and so it asked me how it
could improve them. Its profit and loss account looked like this:

	£
Invoiced sales	6,000,000
Deduct: cost of sales	(3,500,000)
Gross profit	2,500,000
Deduct: overheads	(2,350,000)
Net profit	150,000

The key to improving the company's performance lay in a
number that didn't even appear in its accounts. Its invoiced
sales of £6 million were actually made up of £9 million of sales
at list price, less an average discount of 33 per cent. Discounts,
which were set by the sales manager without any counter-
authorisation, were costing the company £3 million a year! It
didn't take the company long to establish that they could reduce
their average discount by 3 per cent to 30 per cent without
losing any significant customers. By doing this it would save
itself almost £300,000 in discounts, and *treble* its profits from
£150,000 to a much more respectable £450,000.

Is your business giving away unnecessary discounts? How
much higher could your profits be if you controlled your
discounts?

Way 25   The golden rules of discounting

If your business gives discounts here are some golden rules that
you should follow:

- Set clearly understood limits to the powers of individuals to grant discounts.

- Monitor the total level of discounts given as a percentage of total sales value. The best way to achieve this is through your accounting system. Sales should be recorded at list price, with discounts being shown as a cost to be deducted from gross sales to arrive at invoiced sales.

- Monitor the average percentage discount granted by each member of the sales team. Encourage salespeople to use discounts as a targeted tool rather than a universal give-away, and reward success.

- Use selective discounts as an aggressive component of a strategy to attract new clients and generate additional sales (see Way 26).

- Do not allow the business to get locked into low prices because of uncontrolled over-use of discounts for tactical rather than strategic purposes. Remember, low prices very frequently lead to a spiral of ever lower prices – and to an even lower chance of survival.

Way 26 Use discounts strategically

Discounts are at their most valuable when they are used strategically to attract new customers and generate additional sales.

The two principles of strategic discounting are:

- Make sure that you only reward sales the company wouldn't have made without the discount; and

- Present your discount structure in as favourable a light as possible.

Does your business use some form of flat-rate discount scheme, such as a 5 per cent discount on all purchases? If so, I'm afraid that you fail both of my tests for strategic discounting: your discount scheme doesn't encourage customers to buy more than they were planning to buy anyway, and it is boring and uninspiring.

Here's an alternative strategic discounting structure that you might like to think about: offer a 20 per cent discount on sales over and above a target level of sales. Not only does this reward customers who change their buying behaviour, but at a time when your competitors are offering the traditional 5 per cent discount, your 20 per cent will certainly get you noticed.

One great advantage of structuring your discount scheme in this way is that it need not cost you a penny more, provided you set the target level of sales carefully. For example, giving a 5 per cent discount to a customer who usually spends £12,000 a year costs you £600. Giving the same customer a 20 per cent discount on sales in excess of a target of £11,000 will only cost you £200 if the customer continues to spend £12,000. Of course, you hope that the strategic discount will encourage him or her to spend more. Here's the discount they get if they do spend more:

Sales	Discount	Discount as percentage of sales
	£	
Up to £11,000	nil	nil
£12,000	200	1.7
£14,667	733	5.0
£24,000	2,600	10.8

As you can see, the customer needs to spend £14,667, 22 per cent more than they would have done without the discount, before the average rate of discount earned on their total purchases is more than the 5 per cent they got under the old scheme. But the customer is unlikely to object, because the new scheme offers the promise of progressively higher effective discounts as a reward for changing their buying behaviour.

Of course, the key to the success of this type of strategic discounting is to set the sales targets at an appropriate level for each customer. The customer must find the potential discounts attractive, and therefore the sales targets cannot be unrealistically high. At the same time, they must be set high enough to generate profitable and genuinely incremental sales that your business wouldn't otherwise have achieved. Getting the balance right can *sometimes* be difficult, but is *always* vital. Even when you have got it right, you cannot afford to rest on your laurels. What was right this year, may be too generous next year. At the very least, the sales targets built into your discount system should be increased in line with price rises, and ideally they should move in line with the customer's previous year's sales.

You may wonder why I am encouraging you to reduce your prices using strategic discounts, when everything that I have said previously has discouraged price cutting. The reason is simple. Price reductions are very wasteful, indiscriminate and inefficient because they reward *all* customers, even those who end up buying less than before. Properly managed strategic discounting, on the other hand, can and should be individually tailored for every customer, gets you noticed, encourages customers to increase their purchases, and, by careful selection of the sales targets and discount rates, can even *reduce* the amount of discount your business gives away.

Way 27   Overcome discount inertia

Most customers seem to think that they have a *right* to discounts. Once a discount has been given, they expect to continue getting it for years to come. I call this 'discount inertia'.

One possible way of overcoming this is to give all your discounts a time limit: make it clear that they apply for a limited period only, or that they will be due for re-negotiation on a specified date. At least you will have demonstrated to your customers that there is no inalienable right to discounts, and that they have to be earned if they are to be maintained.

But if you haven't put a time limit on your discounts, and you are locked into an inefficient flat-rate discount scheme, or your discount levels are too high, what can you do? Tinkering with your existing discount rates simply won't work. Customers will fight tooth and nail to preserve their current discount rates, and for many of them it becomes a crusade of pride and principle.

The only solution is to sweep aside your entire existing

discount structure, and replace it with a fundamentally different and better one. By making it totally different it is difficult for your customers to make direct comparisons with the old scheme (and if they can't compare, they are less likely to object). And by switching to something like the strategic discount scheme we discussed in Way 26, you are offering an alternative that has a startlingly attractive headline discount rate, and provides some very real benefits to both you and your customers.

Way 28   Settlement discounts

Never offer settlement discounts. Not only do they rarely encourage prompt payment, but once established they are frequently claimed and deducted from remittances even by the slowest payers! They are also unlikely to be very important in influencing a professional buyer. Most professional buyers are judged on the invoice price they negotiate. Settlement discounts are usually regarded as the responsibility of the accounts or credit control departments, and therefore the buyer gets little credit or recognition for negotiating them. As a result, although they will inevitably ask for a settlement discount, it is probably one of the demands they are most willing to withdraw if pressed.

It is sometimes, however, worth offering discounts for cash in advance. Not only can this type of discount greatly aid your credit control and cashflow, but it is often much more attractive to a professional buyer than a settlement discount. This type of discount usually appears on the invoice itself, and therefore the buyer will be able to take the credit for negotiating it.

If you have a customer who insists on a settlement discount, try this strategy. Point out that your standard terms of business require customers to pay within 30 days. Ask him why he should be given a further discount simply because he is going to honour his part of the contract? Then deliver your knockout punch. Explain that the price and discount you have already negotiated is only available if he fully complies with your terms of trade, and that the discount may be withdrawn if he doesn't!

Way 29 A useful quote

Here's one final piece of advice on what to do if price becomes a key issue and sticking point in your negotiations. Try quoting the words of the nineteenth century author John Ruskin:

'It is unwise to pay too much, but it is worse to pay too little. When you pay too much you lose a little money, that is all. When you pay too little you sometimes lose everything since the thing that you bought was incapable of doing the thing you bought it to do.'

Why not use Ruskin's words to emphasise that what you are selling is a long-term, high-quality solution to their needs, and not simply a cheap and nasty short-term fix that the customer may live to regret?

Minimise your Costs

Ask any ten people how to increase profits and nine of them will say 'reduce costs'. I hope this book will convince you that there are many other things you can do to improve your profits, but I can't deny that reducing costs will help.

There are probably only four ways to reduce costs:

• Pay less
• Use less
• Waste less
• Do things differently.

Here are some ideas on how to put these four principles into practice.

Way 30   First principles

Almost every business goes through the annual ritual of budgeting for expenses and forecasting sales for the coming year. Unfortunately, this ritual often misses a golden opportunity. Used properly, budgets are not only useful for monitoring performance, they can actually help to *reduce costs*.

It is important to be crystal clear on one thing, though. A budget that merely takes last year's figures, and adds a percentage for inflation will *not* help to reduce costs one bit. The only way that budgeting will reduce costs is if every cost has to be justified from *first principles* before it is included in the budget.

What do I mean by 'first principles'? You and your team will have to answer the following questions about every single element of your business's cost base:

• Can it be eliminated without significantly damaging the business's profitability?

- Is it over-specified for the needs of the business and could the specification be trimmed to save costs? For example, are you using a Rolls-Royce when a Mini Metro will do?
- Does it cost more than the benefit it delivers?
- Can the same outcome be achieved more cheaply in some other way, perhaps by changing company procedures or by installing a new computer, etc?
- Can it be done more cheaply by an outside subcontractor?
- Can it be done less frequently without harming the business?
- How do other businesses achieve the same result?
- If you were to start in business again, would you still decide to incur this type of cost?
- Is there any duplication of effort, and can the task be combined with one already carried out elsewhere in the business?
- Is somebody responsible for the cost? How do they go about discharging that responsibility?
- When were competitive price quotes last obtained? Has the choice of supplier become a matter of habit and convenience rather than sound economic sense?

Although these questions should be asked about all your costs, it probably makes sense to concentrate on the largest ones first. The larger the costs, the larger the potential savings.

Way 31   Select the product

If the first principles exercise suggests that your business really does need a particular type of product or service, the next step is to find exactly the right make, model or version. Carefully research the options and alternatives. The cost of buying the wrong product or service can be far higher than the ticket price: time will have been wasted, plans and production may have been disrupted and your credibility with customers and staff will have been damaged.

Your research efforts will be greatly improved if you make full use of independent brokers and advisers, especially where they are available on a no-fee basis (as in the case of insurance brokers and independent financial advisers, etc). Don't forget the research that has already been done for you in publications such as *What to Buy for Business*, *Which?* and *What PC?* etc. And don't overlook the research and experiences of your customers and suppliers. Ask them what they use, go and see it in action, and find out if they are satisfied.

Way 32   Select the supplier

Now you know what you want to buy, but who should you buy it from? Think about the things that each supplier is actually supplying. They aren't just offering a product or service, they are also supplying you with:

* Value for money
* Availability
* Location
* Delivery time
* Credit terms
* Training
* After-sales support and service
* Attitude to quality
* Guarantees
* Reputation.

Which of these factors are most important to you? Rank them in order of importance, and assess each supplier against the ranking.

If one supplier is ahead of the field in all areas other than price, point out their price disadvantage and ask them to reconsider. Tell them that you would very much like to buy from them *today* if only they were a little less expensive. This disarmingly simple tactic has stood the test of time remarkably well. It scares the seller into believing that a genuine and immediate sale will be lost unless the request is accommodated.

It is also a good idea to save one element of your required

package to the end of the negotiations. You can then slip it in as an afterthought: 'Oh yes, I nearly forgot, we do insist on receiving 60 days credit' or 'We do take a two per cent early settlement discount, I assume that will not be a problem?' Many salesmen, fearful of the lost sale and the associated waste of their time, will not argue the point. Many of them will prefer to take their chances with the accounts department on their return to the office. I know, I've worked in accounts departments.

Way 33   Swallow your pride and do a deal

What should you do if you can't persuade the best supplier to lower their prices? If they really are the best supplier, you don't have a choice. Swallow your pride and do a deal. If you want *your* customers to pay a premium price for *your* premium products, you can hardly expect to get away with paying rock bottom prices for quality supplies every time. But I guarantee you will get away with it *some* of the time. After all, not everybody has read this book, and not everyone understands that they *can* sell premium products at premium prices.

Way 34   Purchase order systems

A good purchase order system will give your business two key benefits. It will help to discipline your staff into sensible and responsible buying, and it will help you to avoid disagreement and confusion with suppliers.

How good is your purchase order system? Ask yourself the following questions:

- Who can authorise expenditure?
- Are the limits on authorisation limits clearly spelt out and understood?
- Do unauthorised members of staff ever place orders?
- Are unused purchase orders stored securely? One way of preventing unauthorised orders is to prevent unauthorised staff getting access to them.
- Is a purchase order raised for every purchase? Are you sure?

Do a quick audit, and you will probably be surprised and shocked. Get your purchase ledger clerk to send you copies of any invoices that can't be matched to properly authorised purchase orders. While the clerk is finding out whether the expense was genuine, you should find out how the order was placed and by whom – and make sure it doesn't happen again.

- Are purchase orders pre-numbered and systematically filed to enable ready reference and cross checking?
- Do they clearly specify the price, quantity, description, delivery requirements and credit terms?
- Do they make it clear where 'time is of the essence'. This useful phrase can help you to cancel an order without penalty should the supplier fail to deliver on time.

Way 35   Check the delivery

Physically check the quality and quantity of supplies as soon as they are delivered. Are they what was ordered? Is the quantity correct? Are any of them damaged or defective? If you cannot fully satisfy yourself of their suitability at the time you receive them, sign the delivery documents with the words 'Received unchecked'. Check them as soon as possible, and inform the supplier by fax immediately if there are any problems.

Does your goods inward department have the resources to do its job properly? Have you made it easy for them to check deliveries against purchase orders? Do they know what to do if there isn't a purchase order, or it doesn't exactly match what was delivered? Do they have the time, skills and experience to assess whether goods are damaged? Do they produce accurate records of what they have received? Do these records make it easy for the purchase ledger team to check that the business is only invoiced for goods and services it has received? If you can't answer these questions positively, you aren't controlling your costs or your business properly.

Way 36   Check the invoice

It is not enough to control and check orders and deliveries. You must also systematically check supplier invoices as well. Never assume that their invoices will be correct. Even in the age of computer invoicing (or perhaps because of it), it is surprising how often they are wrong. It is also surprising how often these errors favour the supplier! To prevent your business being ripped off you need to ensure that you ask the following questions before accepting an invoice:

- Do the quantities on the invoice exactly match the number you actually received?
- Does the price exactly match the price stated on your purchase order?
- Have any unexpected extras been added to the invoice for post and packing etc?
- Is the invoice arithmetically accurate, including the calculation of the VAT?
- Is the supplier VAT number clearly stated? Don't accept an invoice that includes VAT but doesn't state the VAT number – you may never be able to get the VAT back!

If your supplier's invoices are accurate these questions should take only a few seconds. There are only two reasons why they should take any longer to answer: either your purchasing systems are not working properly, or your suppliers are error prone. Find out which it is, and do something about it. If you don't, you'll never get your costs under control.

Way 37   Easy targets for cost savings

Every business has its own 'easy targets': those areas of cost where it is relatively easy to make savings. But there are some easy targets which are common to most businesses. Here are four of them:

1. *Rent*. The last few years have been a buyer's market for commercial property. There are millions of square feet of unoccupied buildings, rents are falling, and thousands of tenants are going out of business. If you are a good tenant,

your landlord will do almost anything to keep you. This gives you an excellent opportunity to flex your muscles, and negotiate a better deal for your business. One of my clients was recently able to negotiate a two-year rent reduction of more than 70 per cent because he knew that his landlord didn't want to lose him.

2. *Rates.* If you are experiencing financial difficulties you may be able to get a reduction in your uniform business rates (UBR). Although it is rarely publicised, Section 49 of the Local Government Finance Act 1988 allows local authorities to reduce the UBR of businesses in distress. Some authorities are very reluctant to make these reductions, but you won't find out whether yours is one of them until you apply. One thing is certain, you won't get a reduction unless you do apply.

3. *Computer hardware.* This is one area where many companies use a Rolls-Royce when a Mini Metro would do. I run a thriving small business and have very successfully automated all the main business administration tasks with a computer set-up which the computer press would have you believe came out of the Ark. We use one main piece of software, Microsoft Works, a PC based on the aged 8086 chip, and an inkjet printer. The whole set-up cost less than £1000, and has served me very well, doing everything I have asked of it.

The computer world is obsessed with speed, but *you* don't need to be. Does it really matter whether your file is retrieved in a blink of an eyelid, or a thousandth of a blink? Could you use the rest of that blink to increase your profits? If your business is one of the few that would really benefit from using graphically based software packages, such as computer-aided design and desktop publishing, then you may need a 486 machine. But if, like most businesses, your needs revolve around handling words and numbers, you can save a lot of money by opting for an integrated software package such as Microsoft Works and a basic 386 computer. Take it from me, the only time you'll notice the difference is when you are paying for them.

4. *Computer software.* Did you know that there is a perfectly legal

way of getting hundreds of useful computer programs for next to nothing? Many companies producing software don't want to spend thousands of pounds advertising their products. Instead they market their programs as 'Shareware'. For the price of a disk you can get dozens of these Shareware programs for a period of licence-free evaluation. All types of business software are available, from spreadsheets and word processing, to databases and accounts packages. Particularly recommended are the accounts package 'Page', and the Lotus 123 look-alike spreadsheet 'As-Easy-As'. Although most computer magazines advertise Shareware, for a comprehensive guide to all Shareware products try *PC Shareware Magazine.*

Way 38 Outsourcing

Does your business employ people or departments that are not part of your core activities? Fleet managers, tax specialists, travel departments, internal auditors, caterers, etc. How do the costs of having these functions in-house compare to the costs of having them carried out by third parties (outsourcing)? Why not put them out to tender and find out?

It might even be possible for the in-house team, with your help and encouragement, to form their own spin-off business in order to tender for the contract. This arrangement would offer you continuity of expertise and reduced payroll costs. It would give your staff an opportunity to escape unemployment, and to set themselves up in a business they already know inside out.

There are obviously some important detailed considerations surrounding this type of spin-off outsourcing, including the need to satisfy the Inland Revenue that your ex-staff really are in business for themselves. You can't simply take them off the payroll and stop calling them employees. If it were that simple everybody would be doing it to avoid National Insurance contributions and the other responsibilities that go with being an employer. There will have to be genuine evidence that your ex-staff are now in business for themselves, and are taking all the risks and rewards that go with being in business.

Way 39   Try before you buy

I'm often asked, 'What's the best way of reducing my costs?' I usually give my answer in two parts: 'Don't spend any money!' How? 'Get your suppliers to supply you free of charge!' After they've finished laughing, my clients usually admit that while my answer would undeniably reduce their costs, they do have some doubts about its practical use.

But its really not as stupid an idea as it sounds. A great many companies *will* give you their products free of charge. Samples, no-quibble money-back guarantees, items on approval, loans of demonstration models and sale-or-eturn stocks are all examples. Okay, most of them are not free indefinitely. Nevertheless, they can reduce your costs significantly. In particular:

- They allow you to fully test the products for suitability, and reduce the risks of making bad decisions.
- They reduce the costs of buying, funding and holding stocks.
- In the case of sale or return arrangements, they reduce the risks of obsolescence and changes in customer tastes.
- Above all, they allow you to try before you buy. And in many cases they also allow you to sell before you pay.

In some markets these kinds of try before you buy deals are openly available. For example, many personal computers can now be bought with 30–60 day money-back guarantees. In other industries you may have to work a little harder to negotiate them. The higher the potential value of your custom, the easier you should find it. It doesn't matter if try before you buy deals are not the norm in your market. In the current climate companies are bending over backwards to do business. Rarely is it totally impossible to negotiate some kind of try before you buy deal. How many of *your* suppliers supply you free of charge?

Way 40   Paying the bills

When should you pay your suppliers? Thirty days? Sixty days? Ninety days? There is no easy answer. Good cashflow management says you should hold on to your cash for as long as possible. But hold on to it for too long and you may lose the goodwill of the suppliers, and they may never trade with you again. Unfortunately, I can't give you a definitive answer, but I can help to dispel a few myths, and give you a few pointers.

Myth One: Pay early and keep things simple

Giving and taking credit is a fundamental part of business. If it is too complicated for you to handle, you probably ought to be asking yourself whether you have what it takes to succeed in business.

Myth Two: Pay late and you'll lose your suppliers

Yes, if you pay 12 months late you may lose the patience and goodwill of your suppliers, whereas if you pay within 30 days you won't. But there are plenty of other dates between these two extremes that won't seriously damage your relationships with suppliers. There are three main reasons why this is the case.

First, extended credit has become very much the norm in British business. Second, your suppliers probably need you as a customer more than you need them as a supplier, so they will do everything they can to keep you. And third, most companies have different departments for sales and credit control. Just because you've become a thorn in the side of the credit controller doesn't mean that you've lost the support of the, usually more influential, sales manager. In reality, it takes a lot to lose a supplier.

Myth Three: You must pay on the first written demand

All well organised credit control departments chase their debtors in a systematic way. The first written request for payment usually comes about half way through the process. It will normally be followed by several more letters before any real action is taken.

Myth Four: Suppliers can charge interest on overdue accounts

They can certainly try, and some customers may even pay. But they will find it very difficult to enforce their interest demands in the courts. So don't worry too much about the threat of interest charges.

What lessons should we draw from all this?

- Build long credit terms into your negotiations and contracts.
- Never settle your account until the agreed credit period has expired.
- Don't settle until you are fully satisfied that the supplier has met their side of the contract.
- Consider taking further credit, especially if there remains some small element of dissatisfaction (such as an invoicing error), until the issue has been resolved to your full satisfaction.

One word of warning. It is important to pay the Inland Revenue and HM Customs and Excise promptly. As Government agencies, they can and will impose legally-binding charges and penalties for late payment. However, it is still worth finding out from your accountant exactly when they need to be paid, and timing your cheques to arrive *one day before* they become 'late'.

Way 41   If you get into difficulty . . .

Almost every company faces cashflow difficulties at some time. Even profitable companies can temporarily run out of cash. The keys to preventing short-term cashflow shortages becoming a terminal condition are *anticipation*, *action* and *communication*. Well run businesses are able to anticipate shortages, and will have already worked out how to overcome them before they become terminal. Less well run businesses suddenly find themselves in the middle of unexpected cashflow crises, and all too often the experience proves fatal.

Of course, knowing that you are about to run out of cash doesn't actually solve anything. But it does give you the opportunity to act before it's too late. This book is packed with ideas that will help you to plan your way out of a crisis.

One vital thing you should do is talk to your creditors. Don't stick your head in the sand and hope that the problem will go away – it won't! Talk to your bank, your suppliers, your hire-purchase companies, your landlord, your subcontractors. Be honest. Explain the situation. Enlist their support. They have a vested interest in your survival – they want your continued business, and they stand to gain much more if your business survives than if it goes bust. By talking to them before the difficulty becomes a crisis you will have reassured them that you have things under control. Your honesty and candour will be in refreshing contrast to that of other customers, and the chances are they will be more forgiving with your account.

Minimise Your Tax Bill

This book is not about tax. If it were I don't imagine you would have read beyond the first page. But no book on running your business profitably can afford to ignore tax completely – after all, tax and National Insurance will take over a third of your profits if you let them.

There are a thousand and one things that I could say on the subject, but rather than take up 200 pages, I'm going to give you a few of the pieces of practical tax advice that my clients find most helpful.

Because I know that many of you reading this book will have only recently started your own unincorporated businesses, the first four ways have been written specially for you. If you have already been in business for several years, or you run a limited company, Ways 42 to 45 will not work for you, so jump straight to Way 46.

Important note: These few pages can inevitably only give the briefest of introductions to business tax planning. You should check with your accountant before taking any action – there may be technical reasons why the tips given here do not apply in your circumstances.

Way 42   Psssttt . . . Do you want to know how to get 75 per cent tax relief?

Whoever designed the UK tax system for the self-employed had a very strange sense of humour. I think they must have been accountants because they are the only people who really benefit from it. After all, they can charge their clients for explaining the idiosyncrasies of the rules.

Although the Government have promised to make the system more sensible, they can't change anything for a few years yet, and so for the time being we are stuck with it. In a nutshell, self-employed businesses are taxed in this tax year on the profits they showed in their accounts which ended at a date in the previous tax year! Confused? Aren't we all.

The important point to understand, however, is that this offers a golden opportunity to newly established sole traders and partnerships. How do tax inspectors work out how much tax you owe when you first start trading? The normal rules simply won't work because for a new business there aren't any accounts from the previous year. The Inland Revenue's answer is to work out your tax bill for the first two or three years that you are in business using the profits you earned in your first 12 months of trading.

'So what?', I hear you say. But just think for a minute. If your business makes no profits in its first 12 months, your tax bill in years one, two and three may well be zero. Looking at it another way, every £1 your business spends in its first year will save you at least 25 pence tax in year one, another 25 pence in year two, and perhaps even another 25 pence in year three. It is not uncommon for start-up businesses to save 75 pence in tax for every £1 they spend in their first year of trading. In fact, if the business does really well in its first year, and the owner becomes a higher rate taxpayer, every £1 it spends could save 40 pence in years one, two and three. In other words, it could actually reduce its tax bill by £1.20 every time it spends £1! That's what I call value for money.

In a very real sense, the tax system subsidises new businesses. The real cost of spending money will probably never be lower than in those first 12 months.

Way 43   A word of warning

There is one big drawback to the 75 per cent tax relief given to new businesses: it encourages some of them to spend recklessly in the belief that it is 'tax efficient'. For a number of reasons I strongly recommend that you don't let the golden opportunity go to your head, or cloud your better judgement.

Twenty-five pence in the pound is still too much to pay for something that you don't need. It is certainly too much when you remember that you will actually have to pay £1 initially, and then have to wait for months or even years to see the 75 pence coming back to you via a reduced tax bill. And if your business is not going to be around for at least four tax years, you won't get the 75 per cent subsidy anyway (businesses that stop trading within four tax years of starting are taxed on the actual profits they made in each of the years they traded, and are only taxed *once* on the profits made in their first 12 months).

The moral of this is: 'don't let the tax tail wag the commercial dog'. In other words, don't let the prospect of possible tax relief override common sense. If you do, you may find your business running out of cash, time and luck long before the pay day from the taxman.

Way 44 Make the most of the 75 per cent tax relief

There are some sensible things you can do to take advantage of the 75 per cent tax relief without endangering the future of your business. For example, during your first 12–18 months in business you should:

• Hire rather than buy equipment.
• If you do want to buy equipment, it is more tax efficient to buy it slightly before rather than slightly after the following key dates:
    – the first 5 April after the business starts;
    – the anniversary of starting the business; and
    – the date chosen as the business's year-end.
• Borrow money to finance the business for the first 12 months. If you want to you can always repay the loan after 12–18 months. Because the interest you pay on business loans is eligible for the 75 per cent tax relief, this strategy often makes sense even if you have enough money to finance the business yourself.
• Pay salaries to members of the family. Once you've been in business for a few years it usually only makes sense to pay a salary to family members who pay tax at a lower rate than you do. However, in the first year the family's overall tax bill

will be reduced if salaries are paid to *every* member of your immediate family, even those who already pay tax at a higher rate than you. The general rule for new businesses is to pay as high a salary as is reasonable for the work that is done. You'll be surprised how much work your spouse or children actually do: answering the phone, keeping the books, typing letters, filing, cleaning your office, organising your diary, delivering goods, proofreading your letters, evaluating ideas, helping you to plan for the business's future, etc. And because much of this help is often given in the evenings and at weekends, it is reasonable to pay a premium rate for the unsocial hours worked.

- Don't forget to include all the things you spent money on *before* the business started trading. If you are now using them for the benefit of the business it should be possible to claim tax relief on them.

- List all the fixed assets that you are using in the business (computer, car, machinery, desk, filing cabinets, etc). Put a value on them all. If you bought them after you started in business, the appropriate value is the price you paid for them. If you bought them before you were in business, you need to estimate how much they would have been worth on the secondhand market on the day you started in business. For example, if you have owned your car for several years, get a secondhand car guide from the newsagent and find out how much it was worth on the day you started in business. Better still, buy a couple of car guides and keep the one that values your car the highest. These values can then be used to claim capital allowances (the special kind of tax relief given for fixed assets). And remember, the higher the value, the less tax you will pay.

Way 45   When does your year end?

I want to clear up two common misunderstandings about your first set of accounts. There is no law that says your first set of accounts has to cover exactly 12 months, and neither do they have to coincide with the Government's tax year. In fact, for many businesses, choosing the anniversary of the day they started, or choosing 31 March 1993, is just about the worst thing they can do.

Every new business should understand that by choosing its year-end carefully it can reduce the total amount of tax that it pays over its lifetime, and can also give itself longer to pay its tax bills. It all comes back to the way the self-employed are taxed in their first years of trading. As we saw in Way 42, the Inland Revenue base your first couple of tax bills on the profits you make in your first 12 months. But how do they know how much profit you've earned in those 12 months? They simply estimate it from the accounts you send to them. Once you understand this, it is quite easy to take advantage of it – and reduce your tax bill very significantly. Let's look at an example.

Example
New & Co started trading on 1 January 1992. They did very well in their first 12 months, earning £50,000 of profits. The next six months were very poor, and they only earned another £4000, making total profits of £54,000 for the first 18 months. What date should New & Co choose for their year-end: 31 December 1992 or 30 June 1993?

1. If they choose the 12 months to 31 December 1992
   • Their accounts for the 12 months show profits of £50,000.
   • The tax inspector will use this £50,000 to calculate their first few tax bills.
2. If they choose the 18 months to 30 June 1993
   • Their accounts for the 18 months show profits of £54,000.
   • The Inland Revenue usually work on the assumption that the business earned these profits evenly over the 18 months, ie at the rate of £3000 a month. They therefore estimate that New & Co earned only £36,000 in the first 12 months.
   • New & Co's tax bills for the first few years will be based on profits of £36,000, and not the £50,000 that they actually earned.

By choosing 30 June rather than 31 December as its year-end,

New & Co will be faced with lower tax bills. They will probably have saved themselves between £8000 and £12,000 in tax!

Choosing the date to end your first set of accounts is probably the single most important tax saving opportunity available to you. Even if you decide not to use an accountant for anything else, you really must take their advice on this.

Way 46   Reduce your tax bill every year

Once the first few years of trading are out of the way, there are many similarities in the way that the profits of the self-employed, partnerships and limited companies are taxed. As a result there are some tax saving strategies that are available to all businesses. These include:

- Speeding up expenditure on things that you were going to buy anyway, so that they fall into this year's accounts. But it is important to remember two things about speeding up business expenses:
  - You won't reduce your profits or your tax bill by spending money on stock, or by paying for goods or services that you won't actually receive until the following year.
  - The money you spend on cars, equipment and other fixed assets will take a long time to filter through into lower tax bills.
- Delaying some sales until after the end of your accounting period. But be careful, it's not enough just to delay the invoice, you actually have to delay the underlying transaction, that is delay the delivery of the goods or completion of the work.
- If your business operates from your home you can usually claim tax relief for the use of your home. Most tax inspectors will allow you to put through a notional charge of £20–£40 a month in your accounts. You may be able to claim even more if you feel you can justify it.
- If your spouse or children pay tax at a lower rate than you pay on your business's profits, it may make sense to pay them for their services to your business. But remember, if you pay them more than a certain amount a week (£56 for the tax

year 1993/4) there will be National Insurance to consider, and some careful calculations will be needed to work out whether it saves you more in tax than it costs you in National Insurance.

- If your staff want to build up pensions, you will all save money if the business makes contributions on their behalf (in exchange for a lower cash salary, of course). This way you and your staff will save on employer and employee National Insurance contributions normally paid on salaries.

- You can also greatly reduce your tax bill by making strategically timed lump sum contributions into your own personal pensions. If your business is a limited company, the contributions should be made by the company before the end of its financial year. If you are self-employed, or you are employed by a limited company and want to make your own contributions into a personal pension, you should ensure that they are made shortly before rather than shortly after 5 April.

Obviously I have only scratched the surface of business tax planning. If you want to dig deeper into this fascinating and potentially very rewarding area, there is no substitute for taking professional advice.

Way 47   Make the most of the tax help available

Tax inspectors are human. To prove it, here are just six of the ways they will allow you to save time and money.

- If your business's average monthly PAYE and National Insurance payments to the Inland Revenue are less than £450, you can reduce your paperwork and keep hold of your cash for longer by paying the tax quarterly rather than monthly.

- Businesses with annual turnover up to £350,000 can simplify the way they account for VAT by using the Cash Accounting scheme. Not only is this simpler to operate, but it also means that you only have to pay the VATman for the VAT on sales you have actually been paid for.

- If your business regularly receives VAT repayments you

should consider applying to submit your VAT returns monthly. That way you will get your VAT refunds earlier, and your cashflow will improve.

- If you are self-employed and your business turnover is less than £15,000, you don't need to submit detailed accounts to the Inland Revenue. They will usually accept three-line accounts showing single totals for turnover, allowable expenses and taxable net profit.

- If you are self-employed and expect your profits to be quite small (that is, less than £3140 in the tax year 1993/4) you can apply to the DSS to be exempted from the flat rate Class 2 National Insurance contributions. For 1993/4 these Class 2 contributions are £5.55 a week, so you could save almost £300.

- A great deal of advice and assistance is available from the Inland Revenue, the Department of Social Security and HM Customs and Excise. Don't be afraid to ring your local office if you need information or help. They all have Customer Charters and will make a genuine effort to be helpful. For National Insurance queries the DSS runs an excellent Freephone advice line on 0800 393539. As well as answering your queries in person, all the tax authorities have a wide range of free leaflets and booklets, and the Inland Revenue even have a free video they will give to you if you visit one of their offices.

Way 48   Understand the extra cost of non-deductible expenses

Imagine that your sales manager comes to you with a great idea to reduce your marketing costs. His research suggests that if the business stopped spending £10,000 on advertising it could generate exactly the same number of sales by spending £9000 wining, dining and entertaining your key customers. His idea saves you £1000. Or does it?

Unfortunately it doesn't. The £10,000 you spend on advertising actually only costs £7500 because advertising is tax-deductible, so you'll get the other £2500 back from the tax man (it will cost you even less if your business earns enough profits to pay tax at more than 25 per cent). In contrast, entertaining clients is *not* tax deductible, so £9000 worth of wining and dining costs . . . £9000. Far from saving your business £1000, the bright idea costs you an extra £1500.

Businesses that understand what is tax deductible, and what is not, are able to work out the *true* costs of their expenditure, and take them into account when making business decisions. Without this knowledge, bad decisions are inevitable.

Way 49   What is a non-deductible expense?

I have some good news for you. The vast majority of business expenses are tax deductible. But it is still very useful to understand which expenses are not tax deductible. Here are some of the main offending items:

- Wages, salary or drawings paid to the owner of a business (although wages and salaries are tax deductible when paid to the owner of a limited company).

- The private element of expenditure that is part business and part private in nature. For example, if you run your business from home, only the part of your home phone bills that relates to your business activities is tax deductible, your private calls are not.

- Buying, improving or altering capital assets and equipment, such as business premises, motor vehicles, computers, office furniture and other tools. The depreciation on these items is also not tax deductible, although your accountant will calculate a special type of depreciation known as 'capital allowances' that are tax deductible in most cases, and which are calculated at a rate of 25 per cent per annum. Hire charges for equipment, however, are usually tax deductible.

- Political or charitable donations, unless you can demonstrate that they benefited the business.

- Professional charges of a capital nature, such as solicitors' and architects' fees for buying and modifying a new building.

- Provisions and other reserves made for most anticipated future costs or losses.

- The cost of travelling to and from your place of business.
- Business entertaining of customers or suppliers, although entertaining your staff is usually allowable.
- Gifts to customers costing more than £10 in any tax year, or not carrying a conspicuous advertisement for your business.
- Gifts to customers of food or alcohol, regardless of how much they cost and whether they carry advertising.
- Interest on overdue tax, and VAT penalties and surcharges.
- Fines, penalties and legal charges arising from breaches of the law.

Way 50   Shy bairns get nowt!

Only one thing is certain about tax: if you don't ask, you won't get, or as they say in the north, 'Shy bairns get nowt!'. What this means in practice is that you won't get a penny knocked off your tax bill unless you:

- Get a receipt for every expense, however small;
- Record all these expenses systematically and accurately in your accounts; and
- Claim a tax deduction for them at the end of the year.

It is surprising how many small businesses fall at the first hurdle by failing to get receipts, and not recording all their expenditure. Often they say to me, 'It was only £3, so I didn't bother'. But it only takes £1.50 a day to save over £100 a year in tax, so every little bit helps.

The second hurdle is knowing when you might be able to get away with claiming a tax deduction for something which is, arguably, not tax deductible. For example, there is often a very fine dividing line between the tax deductible cost of repairing a machine, and the non-deductible cost of altering or improving it. Similarly, the distinction between tax deductible marketing expenditure and some forms of non-deductible customer entertaining may be blurred. Don't try to claim tax relief for something that is unmistakably non-deductible. But at the same time, don't be a shy bairn (the Scots and Northern English expression for baby). If there are any possible grounds for labelling something as 'repairs' rather than 'improvements', or as 'marketing' rather than 'entertaining', or of taking advantage of any other grey areas between deductible and non-deductible expenses, grab the opportunity.

However, to be on the safe side, if the amounts in question are more than a few hundred pounds you should explain to the tax inspector what you have done. That way, if they accept your argument and give you tax relief, they won't be able to take it away from you at a later date.

Way 51   Keep the VATman happy

Make sure that your business is properly registered for VAT as soon as it has to be, and ensure that your VAT records and returns are prepared in a professional manner. Getting it wrong can lead to very serious penalties and fines which most businesses can ill afford. This is perhaps the most penal area of our current tax legislation, and it is well worth investing in proper professional advice and assistance to avoid the many pitfalls.

Under the current rules your business must register for VAT as soon as one or other of the following two conditions are met:

• Your sales in the last 12 month-period were more than £37,600; or

• You expect to make sales totalling more than £37,600 in the next 30 days.

As soon as either of these conditions is met you must register within 30 days of the end of the month. The registration form, VAT1, can be obtained from any Customs & Excise office. It is also worth pointing out that £37,600 is the *current* threshold for compulsory registration – but it does tend to be increased in the Budget each year, so you need to keep your eye on the Chancellor of the Exchequer.

Not every business waits until the last minute to register for VAT. Many decide to register voluntarily in order to recover the VAT they have paid on purchases. Others register voluntarily to conceal their true size – if they are not VAT registered their customers and suppliers will see at a glance that their turnover is less than £37,600.

Way 52   Beware the bar-room accountant!

Every public bar seems to have one. The self-proclaimed tax expert who declares that you *can* get tax relief for entertaining clients or that it *is* acceptable not to record cash-in-hand sales in your books. The bar-room accountant is adamant that the tax man has never queried his accounts. You ask yourself, 'If he can do it, why can't I?', and you end up concluding that your accountant is either not 'streetwise', or is just plain unhelpful.

The key point to remember here is that just because somebody appears to be getting away with something, it doesn't mean that what they are doing is legal, or that they will continue to get away with it. Some criminals get away with bank robberies, but most are caught and the punishment makes them wish they had stayed within the law. No responsible professional will knowingly encourage clients to break the law, and that applies to tax law as much as to criminal law.

This book is all about equipping business managers to help themselves. I want to encourage you to absorb new ideas from every direction, and be innovative and daring. But I also want to remind you that you must also keep within the law. The schemes of the bar-room accountant are usually on the wrong side of the law. By all means ask your accountant about them. But don't accuse him of being unhelpful or uncommercial when he tells you that they won't work.

Manage Your Assets

This is a long section, comprising Ways 53 to 74. I make no apologies for that. It reflects the importance of the subject. *All* businesses have assets. *Many* businesses waste them. *Few* get the most out of them.

Perhaps because assets appear in the balance sheet rather than the profit and loss account, their effect on profitability is often overlooked. A business that spends 100 per cent of its time and energy on the two most obvious components of profits, sales and costs, and ignores its assets will soon find itself in serious trouble: its machines will have broken down, its stocks will have run out, its staff will have resigned and its cash will have dwindled.

If you want to maximise your profits you will have to understand and manage your assets.

This section looks at four key types of asset. Two of them, stock and debtors, probably already appear in your balance sheet. The other two, your staff and their time, are unlikely to appear on anybody's balance sheet. Nevertheless they are critical to the success of just about every business.

Manage Your Time

Way 53   Are you wasting your time?

How would you react if your storeman allowed thieves to take their pick from your stores? How much stronger would your reaction be if what they stole was uninsured and irreplaceable?

You would undoubtedly sack the storeman for recklessly wasting a company asset, especially if his only line of defence was, 'I just don't know where the stock has gone'. But how many times have you said to yourself, 'I just don't know where the time has gone'. How many times have you resigned yourself to losing and wasting time?

Time is an uninsurable and irreplaceable asset. It is also the most commonly misunderstood and misused of all assets, often because people don't even realise that it *is* an asset of the business. The reality is that time is an extremely valuable business asset which you should do your very best to safeguard. But how valuable is it? Most companies find that when they take account of overheads, the time of even the most junior member of staff costs them 20–30 pence a minute, and their managers' time can cost as much as £1 a minute! How much of your business's profits are being lost with every tick of the clock? How much of your life has sloppy time-management robbed you of today? Are you wasting your time?

There are three key steps to better time-management:

1 Try to understand how you currently spend your time by keeping a detailed diary over a period of a couple of weeks. Better still, get your secretary to keep it for you. You will be surprised by the results.
2 Analyse which of those activities add most value and profit to your business, and which add least. And finally:

3 Devise a strategy to ensure that you focus your time and efforts on the former and not the latter.

Way 54   Prioritise your workload

We all prioritise our workload. The problem is that for many people the basis for this prioritisation is not very businesslike. Very often it reflects factors such as personal preferences, how easy jobs are to finish or simply the order in which work was received.

Ideally, tasks should be prioritised according to the effect they are likely to have on the success of the business. Tasks which are critical to the business's success should be tackled first, however unpleasant or difficult they may be.

One very good way of making sure that you do stick with your priorities is to draw up a *priority action list* at the end of the day. This should outline the tasks that must be accomplished the following day, and the order in which they should be tackled. Doing it at the end of the day has two important advantages. Because you are planning the following day's work, the tasks seem less threatening, and you are not so likely to relegate the unpleasant or difficult ones to the bottom of the list. Some of the emotion has been removed from the process, and the resulting action list will more accurately reflect the relative importance of tasks. Many people also find that by doing this kind of 'diary dump' exercise at the end of the day they are able to go home and completely switch off from work. In contrast, when they don't do it, their evenings are spent thinking about and planning the following day's workload.

Way 55   See the job through

When you decide to do something, persevere at it until it is finished. Constant stopping and starting is a classic symptom of time wasting. Every time you restart a task you have to find the paperwork, remind yourself of the issues and remember what you have already done. This all wastes valuable time. How many times have we all picked up a short letter or memo from our in-tray, read and digested it, decided what we are going to do . . . and then put it back in the in-tray? This is paper-pushing at its worst. Avoid it by handling and dealing with each piece of paper and its related action only once.

Obviously, some projects are too big to complete in one go. But that doesn't mean that you should adopt a stop–start approach to them. They should be broken down into discrete and manageable tasks. Each of these tasks should be taken individually, and persevered with through to completion with the minimum of unnecessary interruptions.

Way 56   Delegate

There is a natural tendency to believe that 'I can do it better than anybody else and, therefore, I must do it'. This is particularly true in businesses that have been built up from scratch: the entrepreneur often cannot accept that anybody else can do their job. Take a long, hard look at yourself. Does this apply to you? Most people deny that it applies to them, but then spoil their case by adding, 'I have to do it myself because my staff don't know how'.

The key is to make sure that your staff *do* know how, and then to make them use that knowledge. Train them, and then delegate responsibility and authority to them. Delegate as far down your organisation as possible.

Obviously, there will be some assignments so important that you will still have to be involved. But even here it is possible to delegate fact-finding and other preparatory work to junior employees, while still keeping the decision-making role for yourself. However, if you do this you should make a point of explaining your decisions to your assistants and, better still, perhaps even allow them to make contributions to the decision-making process itself. Not only will this give them job satisfaction, but it will also help to train them for the day when *they* have to make the decisions.

Way 57   Hold efficient meetings

How often have you sat in a meeting and wondered why you were there? How often are meetings hi-jacked by company politics or larger-than-life egos? How often do you feel that if the meeting had been half the length it would have been twice as good?

Organising formal meetings is an art form that cannot be done justice to in this book. But how often do we actually need formal meetings? My answer is 'not as often as we have them'. In many organisations timetabled and structured meetings have become part of the culture. Rarely does anyone challenge whether they are needed, or whether they are the best way of achieving their goal – communication.

If your business has too many meetings, it is almost certainly not using its telephone system properly. The telephone can be used to replace many meetings. Timely phone calls can nip issues in the bud, doing away with the need to call a meeting later when the *issue* has grown into a *problem*. Telephone discussions are also usually much shorter than face-to-face meetings, because they eliminate many of the pleasantries that are part of the ritual of the formal meeting. Their logistics don't have to be planned with military precision, and they don't cause as much disruption and upheaval as traditional meetings. Telephone discussions get down to business sooner, and get through business quicker.

If you do need face-to-face meetings, hold them standing up. Because they are less comfortable, stand-up meetings tend to discourage pleasantries, focus the mind on the issues and get through agendas at a surprising rate. People don't resent attending stand-up meetings. Because they know that they will not last too long, they don't feel that their time is being wasted, and they are usually enthusiastic to be involved. By harnessing this enthusiasm, stand-up meetings can lead to better decisions.

Way 58   Make your time count

Here are some other practical time management ideas you might also like to try:

- Make sure that you think before rushing into a task. The classic examination room advice applies to business as well: read through the questions and plan your answers before putting pen to paper. If you rush straight into the solution you will make mistakes and waste time.

- If you are not the right person for a task, say so. Don't be afraid to say 'no'.

- Set aside some time each day when you are not to be interrupted by colleagues (although in the spirit of 'customer care', you should still allow customer interruptions). They will soon learn to fit in with your timetable.

- Don't try to do everything perfectly. For most tasks 90–95 per cent perfection will be more than adequate. It would probably take twice as long to reach 99 per cent, and a lifetime to reach 100 per cent.

Way 59   Use call logging sheets

My final tip for more effective time management is so simple that I have to admit to hesitating before deciding to put it in the book. I have included it because it has made such an enormous difference to my own productivity.

I used to frantically search for a scrap of paper every time I received a phone call. Unfortunately, I kept losing the bits of paper. And even when I managed to find them, rarely were my notes sufficiently clear or comprehensive, and I had always forgotten to record some vital piece of information.

You can buy commercially produced telephone notepads. But I find that, because they are usually A5 size or smaller, they are too easy to lose, they don't allow you to make detailed enough notes, and they are not tailored to the exact needs of your business. The solution is simple. Produce your own A4 size telephone notes on a wordprocessor, and keep a sheaf of them in a plastic wallet under your phone. Design them so that they prompt you to record all the information that is relevant to your business. For example, you'll probably want a record of:

- The name of the caller, and the company they work for
- The date and time of their call
- Their phone number and perhaps even their address
- Your rough notes made during the conversation
- Your additional notes made after the conversation
- The action that you need to take as a result of the call

- Whether that action has been completed
- Any other details that are particularly relevant for your business. For example, if you charge your clients for your time, you may want to record the length of the call.

TELEPHONE MESSAGE SHEET

Caller's name: Company:
Date of call:
Time of call:
Length of call:
Phone number:
Date we returned call:
Rough notes during call:

Additional notes made after call:

Follow up action needed:

Call taken by:

Action completed: .... Date .... Signature

---

This type of telephone call logging sheet does much more than just remind you that somebody called. It acts as a *checklist* during the phone call, and is a ready-made *action list* once the call has finished. Because of its A4 size, it is difficult to lose or ignore, and once you have dealt with it, you can simply file it with all your other correspondence. Before long you will be wondering how you ever got by without it.

Manage Your Staff

Way 60   Recruit the right people

Interviewing potential members of staff is an investment in the future of your business. It should not be regarded as an inconvenience, and it should not be hurried.

Never recruit a moderate candidate because 'it's only a receptionist position' etc. Every employee in your organisation must be vital to your business. Why else employ them? And because they are all essential to your success, every employee should be chosen using the highest selection criteria, and should be the very best candidate for that job.

Returning to our example, the receptionist's role can be crucial as the first point of contact third parties have with your business. An unprofessional first impression from a moderate receptionist might lose your business a major potential client. Never say 'it's only a receptionist' again.

Way 61   Use an agency

Recruiting the right person is a difficult and highly skilled exercise. You may be tempted to buy in some of this skill by using a recruitment agency. These agencies typically charge 15–20 per cent of the employee's first year's salary if they fill your position. For a good agency this will be money well spent. But with all too many of them, all you will be buying is advertising in their shop window, and in the local paper. Twenty per cent of anybody's salary is too much to pay for that kind of advertising, especially when there are three million people looking for work, and newspaper advertising rates are open to negotiation.

Make sure you get the best out of your agency. Give them a detailed specification of the job and the attributes that a candidate must have. Only appoint them if they:

- Pre-interview all candidates on the shortlist; and
- Have sufficient confidence in their own ability to find suitable candidates for the job that they are prepared to discount their fee by, say £100, for every candidate they shortlist who turns out not to match your clear specification.

All reputable agencies should find this type of arrangement acceptable. If they complain that it is not the way they usually do business, ask them what business they are in. Are they providing a genuine recruitment service, or are they merely selling advertising at inflated prices?

Way 62   Empower your team

How can you get the most out of your staff? Most experts agree that the answer is to empower them to act on their own initiative, but within a clear set of guidelines. They also say you should monitor the performance of your staff in certain key result areas, identified and agreed with them in advance. You must delegate important tasks to them so that they are challenged and stretched in their jobs, and give them regular feedback on their performance. This feedback should take the form of praise and appreciation for a job well done, and constructive discussion and evaluation of the reasons for poor performance.

People working in this type of environment tend to be highly motivated. The promise of monetary rewards and the fear of being punished do motivate people; but they produce a very limited form of motivation: staff will only do the minimum necessary to earn the reward, or avoid the punishment. In contrast, if you empower your staff there is a very good chance that they will come to love their jobs. Then you will have a team whose motivation and commitment know no limits. And you will get the best from your staff.

Way 63   The 'best' reward package

One of the most important aspects of any employee reward package need not cost your business a penny: helping staff to love their jobs. But very few people can afford to work for love alone. Recruiting and retaining the best people does cost money, and you will have to pay the going rate.

Whether your staff feel they are being paid the going rate depends on how much they value and appreciate the combination of benefits that you are offering, *not* how much they actually cost the business. Can you exploit this distinction to create a win-win outcome? For example:

- Can you offer your staff increased holidays or reduced working hours in exchange for a wage increase that is below the rate of inflation? Many people would welcome the opportunity for more leisure time. The chances are that if your workforce are motivated, or they have some spare capacity, they will cope with the same workload as before. You will have got the same work effort for less money – and from a happier workforce.

- Do your staff fully understand the benefits you provide? There is no point in providing benefits that staff don't value. And they won't value them if they don't know they exist, or they don't know how to take advantage of them. Increase the value of your current benefits by making sure that your employees understand them.

- Was your staff benefits package designed to reflect the genuine wishes and preferences of your staff, or did it simply copy everybody else's? Ask your staff what they want. If any of the current benefits cost you 10 per cent more than their value to your staff, you will probably both be better off if you replace them with cash. If this seems to apply to you, talk to your accountant. Replacing them with cash may result in bigger tax and National Insurance bills, so careful calculations will need to be made before any decisions are made.

In all these examples there is scope for mutual benefit: both you and your staff are better off. Can you improve your employee relations and bottom line in one easy step?

Way 64   Training

Even though I am a qualified chartered accountant, I recently went on an introductory course on bookkeeping. Why? My clients will no doubt be relieved to hear that I didn't go because I needed to brush up my bookkeeping skills! I went because I hoped it would help me to improve the way I explain the subject to new businesses, and I was right, it did.

However experienced or qualified you and your team are, you should never stop learning. If there are still things that can be learnt about the most rudimentary subjects, how much more is there to learn in complex areas?

In a rapidly changing business environment it is vital to identify and satisfy the continuing training needs of you and your staff. Training is not an optional extra to be cut when times are hard, and it should not be used as a management perk. It should be at the heart of your business's culture. To deny that you and your staff need it is an act of gross self-delusion and conceit. To be successful you can never stop learning.

Way 65   Go forth and communicate

Do you talk to your staff? Of course you do. But what do you tell them? The bare minimum they need to know to do their jobs? Or do you communicate to motivate? Used properly, communication can be a very powerful motivator.

Ask yourself a simple question: how many business secrets do you *really* need to keep from your staff? The answer is probably, 'not very many'. Get rid of unnecessary secrecy. Explain your goals and targets, and show them how the business's performance measures up against those targets. Tell them about problems. Encourage two-way conversations. Invite them to contribute ideas, to offer solutions.

If your business has not previously had an open communications policy there will inevitably be some suspicion and reticence among your staff. Initially, you will have to do most of the talking. But once the new policy has become accepted, make sure that you do more listening than talking. Openly communicating with your staff makes them feel involved, trusted and valued. They begin to think in terms of what is best for the business, rather than for them personally.

If you don't think that your business is ready to be more open with its staff, think again. If you're still not convinced, carry out a simple risk-free experiment. Why not give your entire workforce a short presentation on the business's performance? You don't have to give away any trade secrets. All you need to do is simplify the information in your latest published accounts, and explain what it means in plain English.

I recently gave a short presentation like this to the entire workforce of one of my clients. They were all sworn to secrecy, even though almost all of the information we gave to them was on public record at Companies House. Everybody loves to be let in on a secret, and the effect was electrifying. Most of them had no idea how the company was performing. They were delighted that finally somebody was talking to them. This simple exercise was enormously helpful in getting their commitment for a programme of change and improvement. If you want your staff on your side, open up your lines of communication.

Manage Your Stock

Way 66   The two-edged sword

Companies that hold high levels of stock can offer their customers an excellent service. Goods can be delivered from stock within hours, and sales are never lost because they are 'out of stock'. Does this mean that companies should keep their stocks as high as possible?

The answer is invariably 'no'. Holding high levels of stock brings costs as well as benefits. Unfortunately, the true nature and extent of these costs is not always fully understood. They include: the interest cost of money tied up in stock; rent and other warehouse overheads; insurance; shrinkage and other loss or damage to stock; and the risk that stock becomes obsolete or that demand for it dries up.

Complicated mathematical models have been developed to identify the optimal level of stockholding, taking account of both the costs and benefits. What they tell us is that, unless you are in a business where the cost of being out of stock is exceptionally high (eg where one failure to supply jeopardises a major contract), the best strategy is usually to keep the minimum amount of stock necessary to support your normal level of trade. Do you really need all the stock you currently hold? Do you know the true cost of holding it? Can your business afford it?

Way 67   Get stock under control

Here are some practical ways that small businesses can reduce the amount of stock they need to carry:

• Work with customers to get a better understanding of the likely timing and amount of sales. Produce detailed sales forecasts, and plan your production and stockholding around them.

- Speed up the production process. The quicker you can make new goods, the fewer you need to keep in stock.

- Shorten the purchasing lead-time by building good relations with suppliers to ensure priority deliveries. If suppliers respond quickly you won't need to hold reserve stocks of their components and materials. They will be holding the stocks, not you.

- Accept that sometimes you will run out of stock: a business that never runs out of stock probably has too much.

- Minimise the cost and effect of running out of stock by offering discounts to customers who are prepared to accept a slight delay in delivery.

- Form reciprocal arrangements with other non-geographically competing businesses to pool stocks (that is to sell in emergencies to similar businesses who are just outside your own geographical catchment area, at cost plus a small margin to cover handling costs etc).

- Constantly monitor stock levels, and only reorder when minimum trigger points of stock are reached.

- Don't fall into the common trap of ordering once a month regardless of the current stock levels or future sales forecasts.

- Don't be pressured into ordering just because the salesperson has paid you their regular monthly visit.

- Reduce duplication of stocks by reducing the number of stockholding locations.

- Explore the possibility of supplier funding for some of your stocks, for example sale or return, demonstration stocks, evaluation or consignment stock arrangements. Suppliers are often prepared to discuss these kind of proposals in return for some form of commitment to using them as a regular or preferred supplier.

- Remember the Pareto principle. Concentrate your stock controlling efforts on the 20 per cent of stock lines that make up 80 per cent of the total value.

While some of these ideas may be new to your particular industry, it is only by being innovative that you will be able to stay one step ahead of your competitors and your business is able to prosper.

Way 68   Bulk discounts – friend or foe?

Ask any marketing manager: we all love a discount. Used wisely, discounts are a powerful sales tool. But discounts are only wise if they generate more sales than would have been made without them. Take the example of the classic retail offer: 'Three packets of biscuits for the price of two'. If the average customer would have bought two or three packets anyway the discount will be a disaster: it will actually reduce profits. Only if enough customers are encouraged to trade up from one or no packets does the discount stand any chance of boosting profits.

Marketing managers are not stupid. They know that these kinds of bulk discount not only cause customers to *buy* more, but they also cause them to *use* more. Take the case of the biscuits. 'Pipe's law' says that the weekly consumption of biscuits is equal to the amount bought: however many packets you buy, there are never any left at the end of the week (Pipe's law has been rigorously tested and proved in my house on many occasions).

How does Pipe's law apply to business? If you are offered a 'three for the price of two' deal, or any other bulk discount, think very carefully before accepting it. If you were genuinely going to buy two or three units then don't hesitate: your supplier is literally giving away a discount, so take it. But if you were only going to buy one unit at this time, take a few minutes to think about how much the discount will actually *cost* you. Here are some of the questions you should ask:

- How much will it cost to finance, insure, house, control and handle the extra stock? Two to three per cent a month is quite common.
- Is there any risk of their deteriorating or becoming obsolete or damaged?

- Is there risk of a decline in demand for the end-product the stocks are used to manufacture?
- Do you have enough money and space to buy and store the extra stocks, or will buying them mean that you are not able to buy or store something else?
- Will Pipe's law apply? Will you be as economical and efficient using (or eating) them if you know that you have plenty more where they came from? How much more careful will your staff be if they know that it is inconvenient to replace wasted or damaged components?

For many small business buyers, bulk discounts cost much more than the benefit they provide. Unless you are absolutely sure they are worthwhile, don't succumb to temptation.

Manage Your Debtors

Way 69   New customers

Any customer who is willing to buy from you at the asking price is good, right? . . . Wrong! Being willing to *buy* from you is only part of the equation. The crunch question is whether they are willing and able to *pay* the asking price. What's the difference? In a word, cash. A customer who can't or won't pay is worse than no customer at all. And a customer who takes too long to pay may cause you such acute cashflow difficulties that it could prove fatal.

You cannot afford to rely solely on the apparent size of the customer. Even the largest companies don't always pay their debts, and blue chip companies are often the slowest payers of all.

Your best protection is to make proper credit enquiries for all new customers requiring credit terms. At the very least these enquiries should involve the use of a pre-prepared credit enquiry form, to be completed by the customer with such details as:

• Name and address of business and of its proprietors
• Type of trade
• Length of time in business
• Name and address of bankers
• Name and address of two local trade referees.

The bank and trade references should then be followed up. Only when satisfactory references have been obtained should the customer be allowed to place orders other than on a strict cash up-front basis.

Even these procedures are unlikely to be sufficient in every

CREDIT ENQUIRY FORM

Background details

Business name: Contact name:

Business address and phone number:

Trading since:

Name and address of:

1) Bankers:
2) First trade referee:
3) Second trade referee:
4) Owners or directors:

References

Have satisfactory bank and trade
references been received?   Yes/No

If credit to be more than £5000,
have other credit enquiries been
made?   Yes/No/Not applicable

Are copies of these references
attached?   Yes/No

Credit will be refused if the answer to any of these questions is 'No'

Recommendation

Recommended credit limit:

Explain your reasons:

Name: .... Signature: .... Date: ....

Credit limit of £ .... approved by

Name: .... Signature: .... Date: ....

case. For potentially large customers you should contact a specialist credit reference agency such as Dun and Bradstreet and obtain a detailed credit reference. Unless you are very familiar with the information given on these, you will probably need to discuss them with your accountant before making a decision.

Many smaller businesses fear that making credit enquiries will cause offence to a potential customer. In fact, nothing could be further from the truth. All reputable companies will respect the professionalism and good housekeeping of a business that takes credit vetting seriously, and are likely to question the propriety and credibility of one that does not.

Credit vetting is not a one-off exercise. The business circumstances of your main customers can, and probably will, change. Therefore you need to continuously monitor and re-evaluate their creditworthiness. This process should take account of the customer's payment history with your business. You should also obtain up-to-date external credit references. Are they still a good credit risk?

Once you have decided to extend credit terms to a new customer, you should set them a cautious credit limit, and notify them of both the limit and the general terms of trade on which you are prepared to do business with them. Also make sure that these terms of business are stated on your invoices.

Taking credit references seriously probably won't completely eliminate bad debts and slow payments, but it will reduce the risk.

Way 70   New orders

If you follow these simple rules every time your business gets a new sales order you will have fewer queries and will find it easier to collect money from customers.

- Always ask for a written order from a customer, preferably on the customer's own stationery and with an official purchase order number. If you don't have an order in writing they may deny placing it, or use it as an excuse to delay payment.

- Ensure that the small print on the customer's order form complies with your own terms of sale. If there are significant differences make sure they are resolved in writing *before* accepting the order.

- Withhold further credit from any customer who has exceeded their credit limit, or whose account is significantly overdue. Alternatively, make an arrangement to supply them with, say, £50 of new supplies for every £100 that they pay off their account.

- Always obtain and retain proof of delivery for all goods or services supplied. Even if you supply through the post, the Post Office can provide a proof of posting if requested.

- Always ensure that the details on your delivery notes and invoices are accurate. Inaccuracies will not only damage your credibility, but will frequently be used by the customer as a further excuse for delaying payment.

Way 71   Invoice time

Lazy, forgetful, disorganised or worried about customer reaction. These are just four of the reasons why many smaller businesses are often late in issuing their invoices. What they don't realise is that the price they pay for their inaction can be painfully high:

- The longer the delay, the longer it will be before you are paid.

- Customers have short memories. The longer the gap between finishing the work and sending them an invoice, the less likely they are to remember how good the service or product was. This makes them more likely to dispute either the cost or the workmanship, or both.

- Delaying your invoices can also cause you to fall foul of the VAT rules, and you may even be charged a penalty by Customs and Excise.

Give customers your invoices as soon as you have finished the sale. They will still be singing your praises, and you will be paid more willingly and speedily. Why not try to go one step further? Find out their standard supplier payment policy, and take advantage of it. For example, many companies pay their suppliers at the end of the month following the month in which they receive the invoice. Make sure that they get your invoice on the last day of the month, rather than the first day of the next month. It could make a full 30 days' difference to when you get paid.

Way 72   Collect the money

So far we have looked at the kinds of step you can take before and during a sale to improve your chances of actually getting paid. In today's difficult business environment, this will rarely be enough. You will also need to be systematic and ruthless in collecting your debts. In fact, making sure you get paid can often require more effort than winning the original sale. But without this extra effort, the sale is worse than worthless: it has cost the business money and has earned it nothing.

Here are some of the things you need to do in order to get paid:

- Ensure that your debtors listing enables the age of all outstanding debtors to be accurately identified and monitored.

- Review the debtors listing weekly. Identify the risky accounts, and act quickly.

- Chase overdue debts at regular intervals. Once every 10 working days is probably about right. Start by using the telephone to request payment. After the second phone reminder, switch to using both the telephone and letters, progressively sharpening the tone and content of the requests.

- Don't make threats you have no intention of carrying out. By all means suggest to persistent offenders that you will, for example, stop future deliveries until they settle their account. But if you then continue to supply them, despite your threatened action, they will never take your credit control efforts seriously again.

- Keep a log of all 'explanations' for non-payment. Have it with you when you ring to chase the debt, and use the catalogue of carefully recorded excuses and broken promises to shame the customer into paying.

- Send customer statements to all debtors during the first few days of each month. Some companies will only pay on statement, so don't give them an excuse for not paying.

- It is often helpful to bring the problem of the unpaid debt to the attention of the actual *user* of your service or product as well as their accounts department. Quietly suggest to them that you cannot guarantee future deliveries until the account is settled. This frequently ensures that your account gets to the top of the list for the next payment run, as the user's voice is added to your calls for payment.

Above all, remember that successful credit control is essential to the survival of your business. It is not something that can be left to chance, or done by the office junior in between other tasks. Good credit controllers are worth their weight in gold. If you have one, treat them with the respect they deserve. If you don't have one, get one.

Way 73   The factor factor

What can you do if, despite having a good credit controller and following all the tips in this book, you still can't collect your debts quickly enough? One answer is to look at a service offered by all the major banks: factoring.

Factors, as the companies who offer factoring are called, will lend you up to 80 per cent of the value of your outstanding invoices. They will also, if you want them to, insure you against bad debts, and can even take over the day-to-day responsibility for running your sales ledger and collecting cash.

The more you ask them to do, of course, the more it costs. You can expect them to charge 2 or 3 per cent over base rate for the loan. And they also charge for their services: up to a half a per cent of your turnover if you simply want to borrow money; and up to 3 per cent of your turnover if you want them to take over your entire credit control function.

It used to be felt that factoring was a last resort for

struggling companies. This stigma has now largely disappeared. Factoring is heavily marketed by the major banks as a respectable way of managing the cashflow of growing businesses. Another long-standing myth about factoring is that it is only for the big boys. In fact, companies with turnover as low as £75,000 can now take advantage of it.

Whether it makes sense for your business to factor its debts will depend on what other sources of finance are available, how much scope there is to improve your credit collection, and what you will do with the extra cashflow that factoring provides. If you can use the extra cash to generate higher profits then it could be a godsend.

Way 74   Remove the risk altogether

Of course, if your business deals with members of the public you can minimise the risk of bad debts and slow payment by only accepting the following methods of payment:

- Cash on delivery
- Cheques supported by a cheque guarantee card (making sure that you comply carefully with the banks' procedures for verifying the signature and noting the card number on the back of the cheque, etc)
- Credit cards. Although these will cost you 1.5 to 4 per cent in commission, they do ensure that you avoid unpaid debts. They have the added advantage of providing a service to your customers, and at the same time tempting them to buy things they couldn't otherwise afford
- Bankers' drafts or cheques drawn on a building society
- Hire purchase or other forms of third party credit, offered through a finance company.

Business Threats

It always seems so unfair when a leading sportsman has a heart attack. After all, sportsmen are super fit and healthy. They have everything going for them. It shouldn't happen to them, but it does. It is no different in business. You may already be highly successful and profitable, but that doesn't make you immune. There are all too many ways that businesses can become seriously ill. Fortunately, most of them can be avoided with a little knowledge, planning and preventive medicine.

Way 75   Cash is king

Two identical twins ran identical businesses. Both made identical profits. A year later one twin was swimming in the Bahamas, the other was sinking in bankruptcy. The difference was cash. The successful twin had turned his profits into cash in the bank. His unsuccessful brother had paper profits in his books, but nothing at all in his bank.

Running out of cash is the biggest single reason why companies fail. Businesses need profits if they are to *succeed*. But first they must make sure they have the cash to *survive*.

Do you understand why profits and cash are not necessarily the same? Do you know how this could affect your business? Do you monitor your cash position daily? Do you forecast how much cash you will have at the end of the week, month, and year? Do you want to end up in the Bahamas or in bankruptcy?

Way 76   Don't over-borrow

If your business is about to borrow money, stop a minute, and ask yourself why. Is it to buy new equipment, to fund a major contract, to pay this month's wages, or to pay off last month's borrowings? Is your borrowing a sign of success or of failure?

Borrowing to buy new equipment or to fund a major new contract may be a sign of success. But you need to ask yourself whether your inability to generate sufficient cashflow to fund these activities internally indicates that your business is over-extending itself. Have you got the sums right? Is the company heading for a fall? Will it be able to meet the repayments on its loans? If your company is borrowing to pay the wages, or to make repayments on previous loans, it is almost always a sign of failure, and you should be worried.

I am not saying that borrowing is wrong. Almost every successful company does it to some extent. But successful companies also recognise the dangers of borrowing unwisely, of borrowing too much. If you want to ensure that your business survives, I suggest you follow my golden rules:

- Never borrow more than you *know* you can afford to repay.

- When assessing how much you can afford to repay, take account of the worst-case scenario, not just the rose-tinted spectacles version.

- Never borrow to finance projects that don't make sound business sense. The availability of finance cannot turn a bad business opportunity into a good one.

- Don't try to borrow your way out of failure. Borrowing by itself won't address the failure. The lack of cash is not the real difficulty, it is a symptom of a more fundamental problem. If your business is to survive and prosper it must do something about the *cause* of the problem, not just the symptom. It must find ways of increasing its income, reducing its costs and generating more cash. It must find ways of making sure that it doesn't need to borrow. Trying to borrow your way out of failure will probably only serve to speed up the day of judgement. The more the business owes, the more difficult it will be to service its debt, and the more likely are the lenders to decide that enough is enough.

If you don't follow these golden rules you will borrow too much. The history books are full of companies who made this mistake and were forced by their lenders to pay the ultimate price. Don't let your business join them.

Way 77 Don't over-invest

Does your business have to make sacrifices to indulge your enthusiasm for the very latest technology and equipment? Are all your decisions to buy new equipment based on sound economic judgement? Have you rigorously applied discounted cashflow techniques and other investment evaluation techniques? Or are your decisions based on the vague and unquantified assertions that 'the business needs it', or that 'it will improve efficiency'? These types of assertion need to be tested and evaluated, and you may be surprised by the results.

Take a careful look at your existing equipment and other fixed assets. Are they being used to their full potential, could you use them more efficiently? Do you really need to upgrade your existing 386 personal computer to a super fast 486, just because it represents this month's state of the art technology?

New equipment is usually expensive. The expense is often justified, but occasionally it is not. At such times re-equipping can place such a crippling burden on a business that it doesn't survive. Make certain that you can really justify your investment in fixed assets. Make sure you act like a businessperson, not a gadget fanatic.

Way 78 Doing nothing is a business decision – use it wisely

There is one business decision that many managers often don't even realise they've made. It is the decision to carry on as before, to do nothing. The problem is that because it's usually such an easy option, doing nothing has been perfected to an art.

Whenever a business decision has to be made, doing nothing, or at least doing nothing different, is always an option. It is a legitimate and often valuable option. It may even be the right one. But it must be chosen consciously. You must have *decided* that it is the right thing to do. You are not managing if you do nothing by default rather than by decision. You will not make the most of your business's potential if you don't use the do-nothing option wisely.

Way 79   Manage your risks

All businesses face risks. They are an inevitable part of business life. But just because they are inevitable, it doesn't mean they should be ignored. Risks should be managed, mitigated and insured against. But first they must be identified.

Take a long, hard look at your business. Which of these types of risk are you exposed to?

• Fire and natural disasters

• Theft

• Damage to goods in transit

• Your product or staff causing injury to customers and the public

• Over-dependence on key members of staff

• Key staff being poached by your competitors

• Disclosure of sensitive information to your competitors

• Over-dependence on computer systems

• Computer viruses

• Accidental or deliberate loss or corruption of computer data

• Over-dependence on key customers

• Over-dependence on certain suppliers. (This doesn't necessarily mean your largest suppliers. It could just as easily be a small supplier whose product or service is critical to the success of your own business.)

• Over-dependence on one key product

• Falling foul of ever stricter environmental legislation, per-haps leading to fines and clean-up costs

• Interruption to your normal business activities should any of the above disasters strike.

These are just some of the risks businesses can face. How many more apply to your business?

The next step after identifying the risks is to assess them. How likely are they to occur? How significant an impact would they have? List them in order of the threat they pose to the survival and profitability of your business.

There are essentially four ways of responding to these risks:

1 Take action to *minimise the chances* of their occurring in the first place
2 Set up systems and mechanisms to *minimise their effect* if they do happen
3 If it can be obtained cost effectively, take out insurance to provide *financial compensation* should the worst still happen
4 Stick your head in the sand.

Some combination of the first three responses represents sensible risk management. The fourth response is more fitting to an ostrich than a professional manager. You cannot afford to completely ignore any risk, however remote it may seem. But of course, the less likely a risk is, or the less significant its effects are, the less comprehensive your risk management plans need to be. For example, the risk of your business damaging the environment may be so small that your risk management plan may simply involve ensuring that your products continue to be produced using the same strict design and quality control procedures you have always followed.

Have you identified, assessed and managed *all* the risks facing your business?

Way 80   Crisis plans

How would you cope if the unthinkable happened: your premises burned down, your computer erased your key data, there was a major accident at your factory, or one of your products was suddenly found to be unsafe? These kinds of crisis face businesses every day. Tomorrow it could be you and your business trying to pick up the pieces.

You will need more than just adequate insurance to get you through a crisis. You will need a *crisis plan*. Without a plan you and your fellow managers will spend all your time trying to manage the crisis, and the business will inevitably suffer. With a little forethought and a simple crisis plan, you will be able to continue to *manage* the business and, at the same time, *deal with* the crisis.

A crisis plan cannot attempt to be a step-by-step guide to what should be done in every conceivable situation. That would be far too ambitious a project. What it should try to do is to outline the broad areas and issues that may need to be dealt with as part of any crisis. For example, it will briefly explain: who should take overall control; how to deal with the press; how the key elements of the business infrastructure might be restored; and how contact with customers and suppliers should be handled in order to reassure them and enlist their support.

At the heart of any crisis plan is a detailed list of key contacts. Provided it is kept up to date, and a copy is held off-site, this list will probably be a life-saver. Here are some of the contact details it should include:

- *Staff*. It is vital to know how to call upon key employees for help, and how to keep the rest of your staff informed.

- *Alternative premises*. Although it may not be practical to have a definite arrangement for alternative premises, at the very least the crisis plan should include contact names for reliable commercial estate agents and surveyors.

- *Computers*. Details of the company's off-site back-up arrangements, and contact names with hardware and software suppliers.

- *Communications*. Before you can do almost anything you will need to re-establish effective lines of communication, particularly by fax and phone. To help speed this up, the crisis plan should give details of contacts with British Telecom and other telecommunications suppliers.

- *Advisers*. You will need to know how to get advice from your solicitors, bankers, insurers and accountants.

- *Suppliers*. You will need to enlist the support and help of your suppliers, for example in rescheduling deliveries and payments.

- *Customers*. If you are going to keep your customers in the face of disaster, you will need to keep them informed and reassured. That means knowing who to contact, where and how.

You may be thinking: 'I don't need to write all that down, I keep all that sort of information in my head'. That may be true, but what if the disaster strikes when you are on holiday, on an overseas trip, negotiating the company's biggest ever contract, or off sick? Could you be contacted? Would you be able to drop everything? Would it be too late? If it is all in your head, it shouldn't be too difficult to write it down, should it? And if it isn't even in your head, what chance would your business have of surviving a crisis?

Way 81   Money isn't everything

Money makes the world go round. Businesses spend and receive money. Profits are calculated in money. Success is measured in money. Money is a very convenient yardstick. Measuring performance in monetary terms is probably the only way we can hope to calculate and monitor the *effects* of the thousands of processes, actions and tasks that are involved in running a business.

But monetary measures have an important weakness. They are like the speedometer on your car that tells you how fast you are going. If the engine develops a problem, the speedometer indicates that your speed is dropping. But it doesn't tell you what is *causing* the problem. What your business needs is a dashboard full of other non-monetary measures that will actually help you to pinpoint the cause of the trouble. You need the equivalent of a fuel gauge to tell you whether you are running out of petrol, and a thermometer to see if the engine is overheating. If you don't have these types of gauges and measures, and rely solely on the speedometer, there is a serious risk that you won't be aware of problems until it is too late. A minor, preventable condition may have become a life-threatening, 70-mile-an-hour engine seizure.

But what are these non-monetary measures? Unfortunately, I don't know, because it depends on the exact nature of your business. What is critical to the success of one company may be unimportant to another. Here are just some of the indicators that might be relevant to your business:

- Number of customer complaints
- Proportion of orders delivered on time
- Proportion of sales leads converted into customers
- Number of items rejected by quality control
- Staff turnover
- Machine down time
- Your own customer satisfaction index.

What non-monetary factors are critical for the success and profitability of your business? How do you measure them? Is your performance getting better or worse?

Getting the Most from Professional Advisers

Not too many years ago the types of professional service that businesses made use of could be counted on one hand. Today there is a bewildering array of professional expertise on offer. As well as the traditional professions, there are now consultants specialising in health and safety, public relations, quality, information technology, human resources, environmental issues, and corporate identity, to name but a few.

Does your business need professional advice? How can you make sure that you get the best advice? How much is it going to cost? Read on and find out.

Way 82   Take advice

How many small businesses build their own personal computers? I'm told that it is really quite simple to buy and slot together all the necessary boards and components that make a usable PC. So why do so few businesses do it? The answer has to be that they recognise that somebody else can do it more efficiently, reliably and, ultimately, more cost-effectively.

But why do so many businesses fail to follow the same logic when they need professional advice? Time and time again, already over-worked managers get out the textbooks and try to give themselves professional expertise in business law, tax planning, public relations, advertising and a host of other highly specialist areas. There is nothing wrong with trying to solve problems yourself if it is cost-effective to do so. But often cost-effectiveness doesn't come into it. Many managers try to become experts because they are managers, and feel they ought to know about these things. They see it as some kind of intellectual duty. You *do* need to be an expert on the fundamentals of your business, and you *do* need to have a working knowledge of other areas that are important for the day-to-day operation of your business. But you *don't* have to be an expert in every area of professional specialism that your business makes use of.

You already know that it is not cost effective to make your own computers, but do you know whether it is cost effective to carry on being your own professional adviser? External advice may cost you less than you think if you follow the simple rules in the rest of this chapter.

Way 83   Choose wisely

It is all very well recognising that you need professional help, but how do you choose a professional? The answer has to be 'choose wisely'. But how? Cost is important, but it is only one of many considerations. Here are some of the other things you should consider:

- What are their credentials, qualifications and experience?
- Will they give you the names of some of their clients? If they will, you should contact them and ask about the quality and usefulness of the advice and help they received.
- Is their experience relevant? Does it relate to your type of industry, or your types of problem and need?
- Have you met the people who will be handling your affairs? Do you feel comfortable with them? Could you work with them?
- How large an organisation are they? Whether it is better to use a small or large outfit will depend on the size of your business and the role you want them to play. A one-man accountancy firm clearly can't offer the depth or range of service that a large multinational company needs, but a solo consultant in a highly specialist area may be able to offer them all the help they need in that area of specialism.
- Do you want somebody who will tell you what you should do, or somebody who will roll up their shirt sleeves and help you to do it?

- If you already have professional advisers, are they still the best people for the job? Your business and its needs may have changed since you first appointed them, and you may have outgrown their capabilities. Don't let your sense of loyalty to your long-standing advisers stop you from making necessary business decisions. After all, you run a business, not a charity.

- Take extra care when choosing consultants in areas where there is no recognised professional body or qualification. The 1980s and 1990s have seen a proliferation of consultants. Many of them offer a genuinely useful and valuable service, but some have jumped on the consultancy bandwagon, and have little to offer.

If you can find advisers who pass all these tests I guarantee they will save you money, however much they charge. They will give you advice that will boost your performance and efficiency, they will know what works and what does not, they will stop you making costly mistakes, and they will help you to change things for the better.

Way 84   Understand the issues

Before consulting with professionals you should try to get an overview of their discipline, what it involves and how it might be able to help your business. This overview should help you to set realistic goals and expectations for their involvement, ask intelligent questions and understand and act upon the advice given. It will also help you to use as little of their expensive time as possible.

Way 85   Seek 'free' consultations

Many professionals offer free initial consultations. Take advantage of them. But don't allow them the luxury of using the meeting to find out about you and your business without actually providing any advice. You can usually get more out of these free consultations if, before the meeting, you send a written statement of your business situation (a sort of business

CV, explaining who you are, what you do, how, where and for how long etc) and set out the problem/issue on which you need their assistance. In this way they will have had enough time and background information to give the issue some serious thought and the resultant 'free consultation' should actually include some free advice.

If they won't give you any genuine advice before you sign on the dotted line, treat them in the same way you would a shopkeeper who wants you to buy his goods without letting you get them out of the box to check the quality. Walk away.

Way 86   Make their job easier

Professionals sell you their time. The less of it you use, the less it costs. The key to using and wasting less of their time is to organise yourself so that you make their job as easy as possible.

Prepare for meetings. Think through in advance what you want to ask, discuss and achieve. If you try to make it all up on the spot you'll waste their time as you collect your thoughts, and you are bound to need another meeting to cover the areas you forgot. Make sure that you give meetings your undivided attention, and don't waste time by tolerating interruptions. Ask them beforehand what information they are going to need, and make sure it is ready for them in good time. Don't expect them to track down documents and information – it is much cheaper if you do it for them. Keep your business affairs as tidy as possible. Constantly ask how you can improve your 'housekeeping' to make their task easier. If you do all that they suggest you are in a far stronger position to demand a lower fee. I always charge well organised clients less than disorganised ones!

Way 87   Who needs an accountant?

There is only one thing that you *must* have an accountant for: to audit limited company accounts. An audit is a bit like third party, fire and theft car insurance – you are obliged to have it to protect third parties, but it doesn't actually do you much good. Most drivers, if they can afford it, and if their car is worth protecting, pay extra in order to get fully comprehensive insurance. Paying for tax and business advice from a good accountant is like getting fully comprehensive insurance, RAC membership and regular main dealer servicing all rolled into one: it may not be required by law, but it makes the world of difference to the way your business vehicle runs, its fuel economy and reliability and, ultimately, its value. It will also let you sleep more easily at night. Remember, if your car breaks down in the street you may have to walk home. If your business breaks down you may find yourself out on the street with no home to walk to.

Getting the Most out of the Bank

Being a banker in the 1990s is not always a very happy existence. In the 1980s estate agents were widely regarded as the whipping boys of the professional community. Today many bankers feel that dubious honour belongs to them. But whatever your feelings are towards the banking community, the chances are you can't get by without their help. Banks supply vital services to almost every business in the country. In this section we are looking at how you can make sure that you get the best out of your bank.

Way 88   Choose the right bank

The first step towards getting the most out of your bank is making sure that you choose the right bank. It is really no different from any other purchase: it pays to shop around. Here are the kinds of thing you ought to be looking for on your shopping list:

- Are they interested in businesses of your size and type, and with your track record?
- What size of branch will suit you best? Being one of the largest customers at a small branch may give you certain benefits, but it may also mean that your account is subject to very close scrutiny and the local manager may need to keep referring your business to regional managers. On the other hand, being a small customer at a large branch may give you instant access to the decision makers and their specialist services, but, as a relative minnow, the price may be anonymity.

- Can the branch provide all the specialist services you are likely to need?
- Does the location of the branch really matter? For many businesses there is no reason to choose the *nearest* branch. It is far better to choose the *best* branch.
- Don't overlook the personal nature of banking. Does the bank manager understand your business, will he or she be sympathetic to your needs, and can you build a strong mutual relationship?
- How much is all this likely to cost?
- How much better will the new arrangements be? It is only worth changing banks if you are going to benefit from new ideas and services, or from improvements in customer care and costs.

Shopping for a bank is not like shopping for groceries. You can't change your bank every month or even every year. A history littered with too many changes will lead the new bank to question not only your motives for changing, but also whether it is possible to make a profit from your affairs. On balance, four to five years is probably about the right length of time to wait before contemplating your next change.

Way 89   How to get your bank to say 'yes'

All banks like to say 'yes'. They really do. After all, they are in the business of lending money and providing services. But they are also in business to make a profit. They can't make a profit on loans that they believe will never be repaid. Therefore they sometimes have to say 'no'.

Here's a ten point guide that shows you how to increase your chances of a positive answer when you ask for a loan or an overdraft facility.

1 Think carefully about how much you need and the security you can offer.
2 Telephone two or three carefully chosen banks, outline your needs and find out if they are interested. Try to chose

branches that are likely to be able to give you a decision without referring it to their regional managers. In general, the bigger the branch, the more likely it is that they can make their own decisions. But it is probably not a good idea to contact the same bank that you use for personal savings and borrowings – they may eventually apply pressure on you, for example, to sell your house to repay your business loans.

3 Produce a detailed business plan and review it with your accountant. Banks will not seriously consider a proposal unless they are satisfied that:

- Your management team are capable and competent, honest and reliable
- The business can generate enough cash and profits to repay the loan and service the interest
- There is genuine commitment on the part of the borrower
- There is enough security available to the bank should things start to go wrong.

Make sure that your business plan provides reassurance on all these points. But don't lose sight of reality. Your plans must be realistic.

4 It is a sensible precaution to ask for a larger loan over a longer period than you think you are actually going to need. Ten to 20 per cent more money for a 25 per cent longer period is probably about right. That way you will have a margin for negotiation and error, and hopefully will not have to go back to the bank in a few months' time asking for more. If it turns out that you really did borrow too much, you can always earn extra brownie points by paying the loan back sooner than agreed.

5 When you are satisfied with the business plan, produce a very well written, one or two-page summary.

6 Send the business plan and its summary to your chosen banks, along with an invitation to visit your business premises. The chances are that you will be more relaxed, and they will be more impressed, if you meet on your home territory.

7 Treat your meetings with the banks in the same way you

would a major potential customer. Thoroughly prepare yourself. Think about the questions they will ask, and make sure you can answer them.

8 Don't even think about negotiating interest rates until they have indicated the likely terms of an offer. At this point the manager will probably have half to one per cent of room for negotiation over the interest rate.

9 Make sure you understand the nature and meaning of the security you are being asked to give. Offer charges over the business's assets rather than guarantees. If the bank insists on personal guarantees, try not to agree to unlimited guarantees. Instead offer a guarantee with an upper limit equal to the amount of the loan less the other security available.

10 Once you've reached an agreement, get everything in writing and keep copies.

Way 90   Reduce the costs of banking

The days of free banking are numbered. Personal customers are clinging on by their fingertips, but business customers lost their battle some time ago. Fortunately, all is not lost. There are some things that businesses can do to keep their bank charges and interest down.

- Individual bank managers can exercise discretion over the way that bank charges are calculated. For most businesses the cheapest method is a fixed fee per bank statement entry. Small businesses are often automatically offered this method of charging. But if your business is larger you may be paying charges as a percentage of the turnover on your account. Find out how your charges are calculated, do the arithmetic, and negotiate with your bank manager.

- Ask your bank about computerised services such as BACS (Bankers Automated Clearing Services). Because they are automated they tend to be much cheaper than traditional paper-based banking.

- Carefully monitor your cashflow and bank balances. Arrange an overdraft if things start to get tight. Unauthorised overdrafts cost much more than authorised ones, so accidentally going overdrawn can be extremely expensive.

- Bank the cash and cheques you receive daily (unless the amounts are very small).

- Don't have more bank accounts than you really need, especially if some of them are in credit and some are overdrawn.

- Banks do sometimes make mistakes. Don't just accept charges or interest that appear too high. Ask the bank to explain them. If you are still not satisfied you might think about spending about £100 on one of the many computer programs that will double check charges and interest for you.

Something for Nothing

It doesn't take a genius to realise that you can improve your profits if you don't have to pay for the supplies and services you use. But it does take a genius to work out why so many businesses don't make the most of the free advice, training, products and money that is around. How many of these opportunities to get something for nothing is your business taking advantage of? In this section I'll remind you of some of the freebies you might be missing out on.

Way 91   Become a TECcy

Have you become a TECcy yet? Do you know what your local Training and Enterprise Council (usually known as the 'TEC') has to offer? Do you make full use of their services? If your answer to any of these questions is 'no', where have you been for the last few years? Across the country TECs (LECs in Scotland) and Enterprise Agencies now provide free or inexpensive training, advice, ideas and counselling. Some TECs even provide loans and venture capital. Each TEC is independent and therefore tailors its services to the precise needs of local businesses. If your business needs help with marketing, exporting, finance, credit control, quality control, strategic planning, or any other aspect of running a business, the TEC can probably help. If they can't help, they'll certainly know someone who can.

Way 92   Grants – don't take them for granted

Did you know that there are literally hundreds of different types of grant that your business could be eligible for? Quite often the problem is not actually qualifying for them, but in finding out that they exist in the first place.

Here are some of the main areas that may qualify for grants:

- Businesses based in Assisted Areas
- Exporting
- Research and development activities
- Using external consultants
- Training
- Starting a new business.

The best places to start your search for grant funding are your local Training and Enterprise Council or Local Enterprise Company, your local council, the Department of Trade and Industry (DTI) and the Commission of the European Communities. There are also some excellent reference books and computer databases available through most business libraries. Don't be put off if you appear to be getting the runaround. It can be a frustrating process, but the rewards can make it very worth while.

Some of the grants that you should have no difficulty finding out about include:

- *The Enterprise Initiative.* A DTI grant of one-third of the cost of up to 15 days of professional advice from independent consultants.
- *Regional Enterprise Grants.* Small firms in Assisted Areas can get up to £25,000 towards the cost of investment and innovation projects.
- *SPUR.* Small firms developing technologically innovative new products or processes may be eligible for a 30 per cent SPUR grant.
- *The Loan Guarantee Scheme.* This scheme makes it easier for smaller businesses to borrow up to £250,000 on normal commercial terms from the high street banks.
- *The Business Start-Up Scheme.* A modest grant for start-up businesses administered by the Training and Enterprise

Councils. The precise details and terms differ from region to region, so contact your TEC.

Way 93   Make good use of the library

We have a first class library service in this country. As well as traditional public libraries, most major towns now have business libraries. Public libraries usually have a good selection of reference books and trade directories. Business libraries can also offer specialist reference material, international directories and on-line access to computer databases containing information on anything from grants to the financial performance of your competitors and customers. And they will probably have copies of excellent but expensive journals such as Mintel's *Market Intelligence*, that will greatly enhance your desk-based market research. Many of them will even be able to produce mailing lists tailored to your exact requirements and specification.

Visit your local business library and find out what's on offer. Not only will you be able to save money by borrowing rather than buying vital publications, but you will also have access to a much wider range of information than you could possibly build up in-house.

With all this extra information you will be better equipped to mount that next direct sales campaign, penetrate that distant market, raise that additional finance and find that elusive grant. They say that 'knowledge is power'. Are you plugged into the mains power supply, or does your business run on the information equivalent of an AA 9 volt battery?

Way 94   Use the grapevine

The customer care revolution means working hard to supply customers with what they want. Customers and suppliers are now business partners. Why not extend the same principle to information and ideas? Your business partners need information on practically everything from the state of the market to the latest software package, from the costs and benefits of the latest management technique to the response rate you obtained to your last advertisement.

Offer to exchange information, ideas and experience with your customers and suppliers. Most managers love talking about their own businesses, so why not create your own business grapevine? By sharing knowledge you will all gain. As well as benefiting directly from the extra knowledge, you will also profit from having healthier business partners. Fitter customers mean more sales, and healthier suppliers provide a more reliable source of vital goods and services.

Obviously, some information will need to remain confidential, but probably much less than you imagine. Just think of how useful the answers to the following sorts of question would be, and think how little it would cost you to give the same sort of information in exchange:

- What business equipment do you use, and would you recommend it?
- Which business purchases do you now feel were a waste of money?
- What are the practical difficulties of implementing the latest management techniques such as BS 5750 and just-in-time stock control? Have they been worth the effort?
- Have you found any ways to improve your office administration?
- How should we organise our exports? What are your practical tips for the dos and don'ts of exporting?
- Which banks and bank managers should we be talking to?
- Which accountants, lawyers and other professional advisers do you use, and are you satisfied with the level of service and fees?
- What discounts did you manage to negotiate for your recent trade advertisements, and what has the response been like?

If your businesses do not compete with each other, you may even be able to exchange the names of buyers and potential customers. If you do compete with each other, why not swap the names of your lapsed sales leads?

None of this information is likely to be sensitive or confidential, but it could be enormously helpful. So how can you start your own business grapevine? Why not ask some of your major customers and suppliers: 'Can we come and see what makes you such an excellent company to deal with?' Very few companies can resist that sort of flattery!

Way 95   Other low or no cost advice

Here are some other ways that your business may be able to get something for nothing:

- The Federation of Small Businesses offers its members a free 24-hour legal hotline. Annual subscription, which includes a number of other benefits, depends on the number of employees in a business, and starts at £70 for businesses with under five members of staff. The Federation can be contacted on 0253 720911.

- To arrange a free consultation with a local solicitor contact the Law Society's *Lawyers for Enterprise* scheme on 071-405 9075.

- Many other professionals offer free initial consultations. Make the most of their generosity.

- Your bank manager may be able to offer advice and assistance. However, not all bank managers are equally willing or able to provide cost-effective advice, and because their first loyalties are to the bank, they sometimes give advice that is in the interests of the bank rather than of its customers. However, if you have a good bank manager, use him.

- Most of the high street banks offer free banking to businesses in their first year of trading. They also produce some excellent free business guides.

- Advice on your business's health and safety obligations is available free of charge from the Health and Safety Executive. Alternatively, if your business is office or shop based, the health and safety officer of your local authority will be able to provide similar assistance.

- Free advice on whether your business is likely to require planning permission, especially if you propose to work from home, is available from the Planning Department of your

local authority. Alternatively, the Department of the
Environment publishes a free booklet on planning permission
and the small business.

And Finally

Way 96 Work for continuous improvement

No business, however unique or well placed, can afford to stand still. If you don't believe me, take a look at the recent disastrous results of the once mighty IBM.

To avoid going the same way as IBM, you will need to continually review, challenge and improve every aspect of your business. Your products, the service you give to customers, the way you are organised; they must all be continuously improved.

A commitment to continuous improvement means never accepting there is only one way to do things. It means always assuming that there is a better way to do everything, until you have categorically proved the assumption to be untrue. It means being innovative and original. It means taking risks. It means learning from your mistakes, and not repeating them.

The challenge of continuous improvement sounds hard, and it is. But no one said that being successful in business was easy.

Way 97 Everybody can help

By now you should have realised that 'profit' is not a dirty word, it is not a luxury that businesses can do without, and it is not an optional perk for the owners of a business. Profits are the nourishment that sustains the life of a successful business and feeds its growth. If profits fall below subsistence levels, your business will slowly (or perhaps not so slowly) die of starvation.

Do your staff understand this? Do they realise that their jobs ultimately depend on the profitability of the business? Even more important, do they realise that they have a major role to play in increasing the business's profitability, and in securing their own futures?

Every person in your business can contribute to its profitability. Ask them to read this book. Then hold a brainstorming meeting to discuss how the ideas it contains could be adapted to the needs of your business. Get everybody involved. Improving the quality and reliability of your products; becoming more customer focused; handling enquiries more efficiently and courteously; delivering on time; reducing wastage; always looking for improvements in the way they do their jobs; and doing a fair day's work for a fair day's pay are just some of the obvious ways that *all* of your staff can make a contribution.

Don't dismiss any of the brainstorming ideas out of hand, however small a contribution they may appear to offer. Small changes can have very big effects. I was recently able to show a company how four small improvements of 1 per cent in costs, prices, discounts and sales volumes would enable it to quadruple its net profits. In many ways, 'small is beautiful' because it is usually much easier and quicker to make a series of small improvements than a single, major one.

Is your entire team pulling in the same direction? Are they all striving to achieve greater profitability?

Way 98   Break the mould

Most of us don't realise how conventional we are. Whether we are aware of it or not, we tend to think and work within a very narrowly defined set of rules. These rules and conventions stifle initiative, innovation and change. They prevent us from making the most of our opportunities.

If you don't believe this applies to you, try a simple puzzle. Can you join up all nine dots in the diagram below using four straight lines, but without taking your pencil off the page, and without doubling back on yourself?

Unless they've seen the puzzle before, most people can't solve it because they think conventionally. They try to draw all their four lines inside the box. But there is nothing in the puzzle that says you can't go beyond the bounds of the box. In fact, as you can see below, the only way to solve the puzzle is to break out of the box.

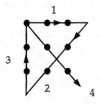

In many ways the puzzle symbolises the way we usually approach business problems and challenges. We unknowingly superimpose a box of conventional thinking over our problems, making them much harder to solve. Open up your mind to new ideas, actively encourage new ways of doing things, think laterally and break out of the box. You'll be amazed at how much easier solving problems and making profits can become.

Way 99 An expert in a box

Computer software is the twentieth century's equivalent of the genie in the lamp. Instead of rubbing a lamp, we insert a floppy disk. If you insert the right disk you might not get a genie, but you will get the genius of some very experienced company doctors, consultants and academics who are all experts in improving the profits of small and medium-sized companies.

Durham University Business School have helped to develop an expert computer program called *Profitwise* that can help to diagnose the causes of low or unsatisfactory profitability, and provides advice and action plans tailored to your circumstances. It won't solve all your problems or tell you everything you need to know, but it is extremely comprehensive and easy to use, and will point you in the right direction.

Ask your local Training and Enterprise Council, Local Enterprise Company or Enterprise Agency if they use *Profitwise*. If they don't you can find out more about the program by ringing Headway Systems on 0457 860363. You may even decide to buy your own expert in a box!

Way 100   Don't put this book down

If you've read the book this far you've probably already recognised 20 or 30 things that you can do to improve the profitability of your business. But don't fool yourself. It's not enough to have *identified* room for improvement. You have actually got to make those improvements *happen*. All too often the good intentions and ideas that people take away from courses and books are never converted into action. They are filed at the bottom of an in-tray, and swallowed up by the pressures of work. If you are managing your business, you have a duty to find time to manage its profits and its future. You are failing as a manager if you let your ideas languish in the filing system.

Don't put this book down until you have listed at least five steps you are going to take *today* to improve your profits, and ten more things you are going to do *tomorrow*.

Improving your profits today:

1

2

3

4

5

Improving your profits tomorrow:

1

2

3

4

5

6

7

8

9

10

Way 101 If all else fails

What can you do if you have tried all the ideas in this book, and your profits are still not what you would like them to be? You might find the answer in 'creative accounting'.

Creative accounting is the art of making your profits look better than they really are. It can be extremely useful in persuading suppliers to give you credit, persuading bankers to offer you a facility, and in persuading customers that you are a business worth dealing with.

The accounting profession is working hard to outlaw many of the most sophisticated methods of creative accounting used by large companies. But there are still some simple techniques which are perfectly legitimate. For example:

- Reassess the expected life of your fixed assets, and their value at the end of their useful life. If possible, reduce the depreciation charged in your profit and loss account.

- Reassess your general exposure to bad debts and stock obsolescence. If there are any grounds for optimism, reduce the percentage rates used to calculate general provisions.

- Ask your accountant if your business has any assets which don't appear on its balance sheet. Putting them on the balance sheet might reduce the costs that you have to show in your profit and loss account.

AND FINALLY

There are two golden rules for using creative accounting:

- Don't do anything that is illegal or contravenes generally accepted accounting practice; and above all:
- Don't fool yourself into believing that your profits really have improved!

Index